the journal of strange phenomena

WEIRD WORLD

1999

Edited by Mark Pilkington & Joe McNally

Published by John Brown Publishing Ltd.

The New Boathouse, 136 – 142 Bramley Road, London W10 6SR

fortean times
the journal of strange phenomena

WEIRD WORLD 1999

Edited by Mark Pilkington & Joe McNally

General Editor: John Innes
Design: Keith Jackson

Cover Design: Button
Picture Research: Christine Wood
Managing Editor: Jane Watkins
Contributors: Bob Rickard, Paul Sieveking, Ian Simmons, Mike Dash, Rev. Lionel Fanthorpe, Ted Harrison, Jonathan Downes, Bruce Wright, Mark Chorvinsky, Andrew Green and Rob Irving

First published in Great Britain in November 1998
By JOHN BROWN PUBLISHING, The New Boathouse, 136-142 Bramley Road, London, W10 6SR
Tel 0171 565 3000 Fax 0171 565 3050

(c) Fortean Times/John Brown Publishing 1998

HOW TO FIND COPIES OF FORTEAN TIMES

FORTEAN TIMES is on sale monthly in most large newsagents. You can also order copies to be reserved for you in outlets which do not presently stock the magazine.

To order a sample copy or for details of subscriptions
☎ 01454 620070

In the United States
☎ (800) 221 3148

British Library Cataloguing in Publication Data available
ISBN 1-902212-002

Printed and bound in Great Britain by
Butler & Tanner Ltd, Frome and London

WEIRD WORLD

CONTENTS

KEITH JACKSON

ALEX HOWE

AP

PHIL BOND

www.arttoday.com

www.arttoday.com

PHIL BOND

THE**PARANORMAL**WORLD

STEPHEN ALEXANDER

THE**NATURAL**WORLD

NASA

www.arttoday.com

NASA

DOGGONE CRAZY

THIS SCULPTURE by Robert Bradford at Hardcastle Crags, near Hebden Bridge, West Yorkshire, is entitled "Cabot's dog waiting patiently for his master to return from the high seas". It is part of a trail designed to encourage visitors to make art from their surroundings. *D.Telegraph, 23 June 1998.*

PHOTO: WILL LACK

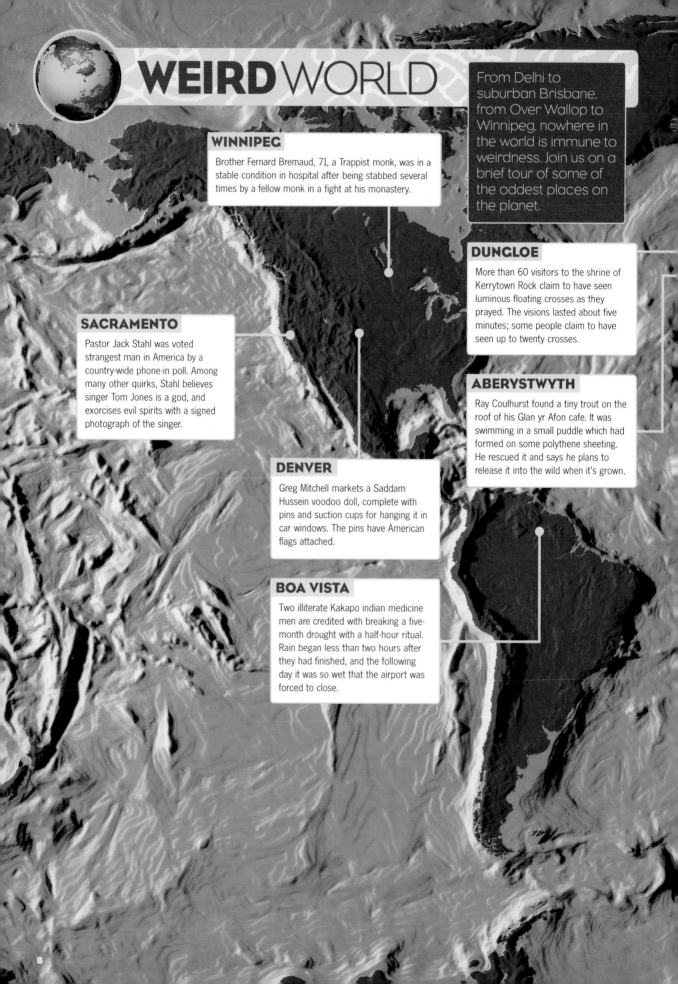

WEIRD WORLD

WINNIPEG

Brother Fernard Bremaud, 71, a Trappist monk, was in a stable condition in hospital after being stabbed several times by a fellow monk in a fight at his monastery.

DUNGLOE

More than 60 visitors to the shrine of Kerrytown Rock claim to have seen luminous floating crosses as they prayed. The visions lasted about five minutes; some people claim to have seen up to twenty crosses.

SACRAMENTO

Pastor Jack Stahl was voted strangest man in America by a country-wide phone-in poll. Among many other quirks, Stahl believes singer Tom Jones is a god, and exorcises evil spirits with a signed photograph of the singer.

ABERYSTWYTH

Ray Coulhurst found a tiny trout on the roof of his Glan yr Afon cafe. It was swimming in a small puddle which had formed on some polythene sheeting. He rescued it and says he plans to release it into the wild when it's grown.

DENVER

Greg Mitchell markets a Saddam Hussein voodoo doll, complete with pins and suction cups for hanging it in car windows. The pins have American flags attached.

BOA VISTA

Two illiterate Kakapo indian medicine men are credited with breaking a five-month drought with a half-hour ritual. Rain began less than two hours after they had finished, and the following day it was so wet that the airport was forced to close.

LOCH NESS

A Glasgow woman staying near the Loch was awoken by a flock of geese, and heard a weird humming noise which scared her so badly she couldn't leave her tent until dawn. The hum was heard close to where an angler had seen a "large black beast with a head like a rhino".

SWEDEN

A couple who were fined £390 and told to find a shorter name when they called their son Bfxxccxxmnpckccc111mmnprxvc1mnckssqibb1111 6 (pronounced "Albin") have upset the authorities again by registering the child as "A".

FRANKFURT

Nanny Elizabeth Decastro, from Manila, boarded her plane to London as normal, but never got off at Heathrow. Detectives and airline alike are at a loss to explain it.

KAZAKHSTAN

Hundreds of expensive silk shirts imported from China were burned after a red powder in the buttons sparked a health scare. In fact, it was naphthalene to deter moths.

DELHI

A one-day Conference of Fools was held on 13 March, to show "that people with no malice do no harm"

ITALY

Three con-men were jailed for 30 months after they convinced an elderly couple to give them over £220,000 to buy uranium to feed an "extraterrestrial doctor" who, they said, would cure the couple of all their ills.

HONG KONG

Students at the island's university were baffled as to why the statue on the campus commemorating the dead of Tiananmen Square didn't seem to have any Asian faces on it. Eventually, they found out it had been created in memory of the dead of the Oklahoma bomb, but the US Government had turned it down.

EGYPT

A buffalo with two heads, two tails and seven feet was born in the northern province of Daqahliya. The vet who assisted in the birth blamed the deformities on pesticides.

COLOMBO

As he was asked into the witness box, Subhasinghe Premasiri, charged with theft, produced a plastic bag filled with dung and threw it at a policeman. It missed, and hit a fan, showering the contents over all present.

SOUTH AFRICA

President Mandela was stung several times on the stomach and privates by a swarm of angry bees. Local healers felt that the president's ancestors were sending him a warning.

BRISBANE

A man of 63 was arrested after allegedly breaking into the home of an 83-year-old woman in Yeronga, on the outskirts of the city. She woke at about 5am on 31 January when she felt someone licking her face. The man fled when she screamed.

Top 10 Weird People

❶ SOFA SLASHER

LUCIA R., a 64-year-old Dutch woman known as the "furniture terrorist", was jailed for eight months for slashing sofas in furniture showrooms with a razor blade. Over a period of six years, she caused damage estimated at £300,000, cycling to south Holland and north Belgium to rip open cushions and carve on table-tops.

❷ CHEST INJURIES

PHYSICAL THERAPIST Paul Shimkonis took the Diamond Dolls Club of Clearwater, Florida to court after allegedly suffering whiplash induced by the 69HH breasts of porn star Tawny Peaks. Friends of Shimkonis had paid for Peaks to massage his face with her mammaries. On American TV's *The People's Court* Shimkonis said; "It felt like two cement blocks hit me." But a court officer who examined Peaks' assets disagreed; "They were not as dense as the plaintiff described. They were soft." *The People's Court* ruled in favour of Peaks and the club.

❸ SHOE HORNY

28-YEAR-OLD Ross Watt was fined £100 in Edinburgh for shameless indecency. Watt had been discovered outside Hawkhill Court early one morning with his trousers down. He was lying on top of a shoe and was reportedly simulating sexual intercourse with it.

❹ LEVEL CROSSING

A WOMAN was detained at the Latvian-Russian border after guards found that she was emitting radiation 10 times the admissible level. She was released after explaining that this was due to treatments at the local medical centre for thyroid cancer. This begs the question of why the border guards were checking in the first place.

❺ SCORPION ORDEAL

IN JULY, Malaysian snake charmer Ali Khan Samsudin branched out and spent 21 days in a glass cage with 6,000 venomous scorpions to break the official world record of 15 days. He was stung around a hundred times but was reportedly "hale, hearty and very fit" at the end of his ordeal. He began with only 5,000 scorpions in the cage, but on the eleventh day, a spectator threw in another thousand gathered from the wild, claiming that the ones inside the cage weren't venomous. Khan attributed his survival to the herbs he ate each day. He comes from a long line of snake-charmers, and previously sat with 400 cobras for twelve hours every day for forty days.

6 THE MAN WHO SOLD THE MOON

DENNIS HOPE, of Rio Vista, California, has proclaimed himself Master of the Solar System, a title which he says gives him claim to every planet, satellite and asteroid in our solar system, with the exception of Earth. And since he owns it all, he has now begun to sell it. Hope claims to make some $4,000 (£2,530) a month from selling off plots of land on the Moon, which he says is "the least expensive real estate in the universe" at $15.99 (£10) plus tax and shipping for 1,777 acres of prime lunar property. "Whenever someone hears of this," he says, "their first response is 'You can't do that.' Well, we've sold over 10,000 parcels of land, so evidently, I can."

7 TONGUE TWISTER

CHINESE SURGEONS operated on a man with three tongues, removing two of them so he can talk and eat normally for the first time in 20 years. Xian Shihua, a 32-year-old peasant from the province of Sichuan, was born with one tongue, but a second, smaller one grew when he was five years old, with the third appearing later. The largest of the three tongues was 13in (33cm) long, 6in (15cm) wide and 4.4in (11cm) thick. The other two were 3.6in (9cm) long and of varying widths and thicknesses. The operation at the South-west Military Hospital in Chongqing city finally enabled him to go off the liquid diet on which he has had to subsist since childhood.

8 GOD'S SALVATION CHURCH

IN MARCH, hundreds of members of a UFO cult known as God's Salvation Church assembled in the Texas town of Garland to await the return of Jesus. The Saviour was due to reincarnate in the form of the cult's leader, Dr Chen Hon-Ming, then "clone" himself thousands of times so he could shake hands with all those present. Television channels the world over would spontaneously begin to broadcast images of the cult's headquarters a week before the Second Coming. Unfortunately Jesus failed to turn up.

9 AWAY WITH THE FAIRIES

TELEVISION VIEWERS in the Netherlands were surprised to see their Deputy Director-General for the Environment admit in a television interview that he believed in fairies. He elaborated three days later in a newspaper interview, where he asserted belief in gnomes, dwarves, elves, tree spirits, and "landscape angels". Gnomes, he explained, "are a few decimetres tall," while elves are much smaller. "Landscape angels", meanwhile, are "metres tall" and "composed of various colours".

10 OFF THEIR TROLLEYS

SUPERMARKETS APPEAR to attract odd behaviour. A woman who bought a pack of 100 cotton buds from Sainsbury's wrote to complain that one was missing. She explained that she had planned to buy her next box three months later, on the 30th of the month. "My restocking plans have gone right out the window" she wrote. "As I am due to be at work on the 29th, I will have to take a day's holiday to go shopping." Another woman complained that store staff had deliberately pushed a trolley at her, injuring her; she warned that if her damages claim was not met she would redirect the necessary forces from Japan to create an earthquake in Britain and take control of the Crown Jewels.

FABRICE

FLIRTING WITH LADY LUCK

☺ **THE BRITISH** *Medical Journal* told the remarkable story of a woman – identified only as AB – with a history of psychological problems. While at home reading, AB heard a voice tell her not to worry, that it was a friend. She sought medical advice, and was apparently cured after counselling and medication. However, the phenomenon recurred while she was on holiday. This time, two voices told her to return to England immediately, as there was something wrong. Once in London, the voices gave her an address, which turned out to be the brain scan department of a large London hospital. She told doctors that the voices said she had a brain tumour and an inflamed brain stem.

Doctors decided to carry out the scans to prove that nothing was wrong. However, on examination, the pictures did indeed reveal a tumour. After surgery, AB reported that she only heard the voices once more; they told her; "We are pleased to have helped you. Goodbye," and fell silent, apparently forever.

☺ **ELDON FERGUSON**, 44, was flying with a friend in a hired Cessna from Quebec to Newfoundland when an explosion blew off the front of the aircraft. He fell 5,000ft (1,524m) and landed unhurt in a snow drift. Both pilots were killed.

☺ **"BANKS" IS** not just the most appropriate, but also the most common name for winners of Littlewoods' Lotteries scratchcards, beating off Smith, Jones and Brown, according to a survey. Meanwhile, in Bordeaux, France, M. and Mme. Lotterie were not surprised by a £1 million lottery win.

☺ **DARREN GARSIDE**, 15, touched a mains electricity cable while rescuing four-year-old Jay Nother from a hole dug by workmen. He was flung 9ft (2.7m) through the air and suffered severe burns to his face, left arm and back; his life was saved by the thick rubber soles on his trainers. After being released from Salisbury District Hospital, he found that his acne was cured. "I used to have spots all over my face," he said, "but now the skin has peeled off, and they've all gone.

As the poet said, we are to the gods of fate as flies to wanton children; they play with us as they will. These next two pages certainly seem to prove the point; sometimes it seems that the universe really has it in for one person while desperately wanting to protect another...

CONSTRUCTION WORKER Andrew Jepson, 26, survived being run over by a four-ton steamroller. The roller was reversing at a noisy building site at Heathrow Airport and caught Jepson's leg while his attention was distracted. He could not escape and the machine rolled over his entire body, face down. The driver accelerated the roller to the maximum 7mph (11km/h) to ensure it was on top of his colleague for the minimum time. He was saved by his hard hat and the uneven surface of pebble, shale and mud, the foundation for a road. He remained fully conscious and escaped with crushed ribs, bruising, cuts and a collapsed left lung. He spent two days in intensive care, but six days later was allowed home. The accident bore a strange resemblence to the climax of the film *A Fish Called Wanda*, where an enraged Michael Palin runs over his partner in crime, Kevin Kline, with a steamroller at Heathrow; Kline survives because he is being pressed into wet concrete.

KOBAL

O UNLUCKY MAN!

Unfortunately luck comes in two kinds, good and bad. Here are some stories from the latter...

☹ On the first Friday 13th of the year, in February, Dick Whisson got stuck in a lift in the British Telecom office in Chatham, Kent, while putting up a notice telling people what to do if they got stuck in the lift. He had to wait an hour and a half to be freed by local firefighters because BT's lift engineers were in Bristol.

☹ A 550lb (227kg) RAF bomb dropped on Stadtlohn, near Essen, Germany, during World War II detonated under Bernhard Lindner's back garden, wiping out his prized collection of garden gnomes. The blast blew up his garage and left a 10ft (3m) crater in his lawn. The detonation was blamed on a change in ground water levels.

☹ A middle-aged phsyiotherapist had every one of her ribs broken when she was attacked by a herd of cows while walking her dog in a field near Bloxham, Oxfordshire. Helen Cowmeadow also suffered a broken collar bone and punctured lung, yet managed to stagger 600 yards (550m) to get help.

☹ A British tourist who stole a lump of stone from the base of the Giza pyramid as a souvenir five years ago returned it to the Egyptian authorities saying it had brought "bad luck ever since". In a letter to the Egyptian museum in Cairo, the tourist said, "I was a fool to take it and I am very sorry."

☹ As if to show that good luck can't last, Chilean police officer Hector Cuevas became a national celebrity in 1995 when he was shot at close range by an armed bank robber. The robber's bullet was stopped by a pen in Cuevas' pocket, and he suffered nothing more damaging than a dirty shirt. Years later, a eucalyptus tree fell on his squad car and crushed him to death.

SAFETY OFFICER David Spear, 38, of Penarth, Cardiff, has not had much luck, expecially when it comes to emergency vehicles. While watching a neighbourhood dispute in his road, he was knocked down by a police car racing to the scene. His injuries were not serious, but a year later he was walking home from the pub when he was mown down by a 22-ton fire engine. "I woke up in hospital four weeks later after being in a coma," he said. "I had broken just about every bone in my body, and doctors said I'd never walk again."

He proved them wrong and three years later he was walking home from the paper shop one winter morning when he slipped on some ice and was knocked unconscious. He came round as he was being stretchered into an ambulance. On the way to casualty, the ambulance skidded on black ice and crashed. Mr Spear broke his neck and spent another six weeks in hospital.

The safety officer has always been accident prone. He has fallen off ladders, tripped into a swimming pool and fallen head-first into a cesspit. "I don't have to stray far from my front door before something goes wrong," he said. "I swung a rubbish bag into the back of the local bin lorry, but caught my finger in the knot and couldn't let go. The bag became trapped in the crusher and I ended up tearing all the tendons in my hand. I then fell flat on my face in the road and broke my nose."

DR CHEN

UP TO NO GOD IN TEXAS

The "saucer cult" led by Dr Chen Hon-Ming suffered something of a setback in March. The group, known variously as the God's Salvation Church, God Saves The Earth Flying Saucer Foundation, and Chen Tao, anticipated that God would physically incarnate in Chen's body on March 31st, after a remarkable series of miracles and signs. Sadly, it failed to happen.

As the deadline approached, they declared that one week beforehand – March 24th – all the televisions in America would spontaneously begin to broadcast messages of support for Chen and co. God was expected to tune the nation's TVs to Channel 18 and speak over pictures of the group's base in Garland, Texas.

Spokesman Richard Liu explained that on March 31st, God would physically assume Chen's outward appearance, clone himself and address the world over their TVs. Six days later, he would physically manifest at the group's Riverside Drive base, where he would provide proof of his divinity by walking through walls, cloning himself thousands of times so he can shake hands with everybody, and answering questions put to him in any language. According to the group's beliefs, these events would precede the Great Tribulation, a nuclear holocaust which they expected to erupt in Asia and eventually bring about the end of the world in 2043.

However, March 24th came and went without event. To his credit, Dr Chen seemed to take it reasonably well; there had been a number of hysterical articles in the local and world press as the date approached, suggesting that – despite the group's constant insistence to the contrary – a Heaven's Gate-style mass suicide was in the offing. The local police placed a wide cordon around their base and went so far as to mobilise an extra 50 police officers and emergency personnel. In the event, Chen simply opened the door of the Riverside Drive HQ and, rather sheepishly, apologised. With a candour that other apocalyptic groups would do well to emulate, he told the assembled crowd of reporters that "since God's appearance on television has not been realised, you can take what we have preached as nonsense. I would rather you don't believe what I say any more."

The cult first came to our attention in 1997, when Chen – a pharmacology instructor – camped out for several days at Vancouver airport awaiting "the Jesus of the West". In their rather involved cosmology, the Western Jesus was due to rendezvous with the Eastern Jesus, a nine-year-old boy called Lo Chi-Jen, who accompanied them on their travels. The two would then proceed to nearby Burnaby Lake, where they would meet up with the original Jesus. Although the Western Jesus failed to appear, Chen was confident enough to describe him as an Abraham Lincoln look-a-like born in Vancouver in late 1969 and standing some 6ft (1.8m) tall.

After a number of obviously unsuitable candidates presented themselves – including a large man who said he was called "Abraham", held a staff above his head and shouted "shalom" several times – they gave up and decamped to the lake anyway. Subsequently, they migrated to Garland, chosen because in Chen's heavily-accented English, the name resembled "God-Land".

THE CULT OF ELVIS

Elvis may have popped his blue suede shoes, but for many his spirit never left the building. TED HARRISON looks at people who've got the fever.

"I found myself in Paradise and suddenly I saw this all but blinding white light and heard a voice came out of the light saying, 'go back and tell them, Elvis'".

Texan Robert Campbell remembers his vision vividly. From that moment he became a changed man dedicated to telling the world that Elvis Presley, and not Jesus, had been the true Messiah, that the Bible stories of Jesus were not history but prophecy foretelling the king of rock 'n' roll and that Elvis would shortly return to judge the world.

His belief in Elvis's messianic role is not unique. Thousands of his fans find religious meaning in Presley's life and music and hundreds of them share Robert Campbell's dedication to Elvis as a man of divine and apocalyptic destiny.

Fans pour over every detail of Elvis's life to find coincidences of significance. Some have likened Elvis's jewelled jumpsuit to the clothes described in the Old Testament to be worn by the priests of Israel. And who,

they ask, was the first priest of Israel? And what was Elvis's middle name? Aaron is the answer on both counts.

A trawl through the internet reveals several Elvis churches. "Welcome to the only religion that will matter in the next millennium," boasts the First Presleytarian Church of Elvis the Divine. And the internet iconography is as revealing as it is startling or, to believing Christians, blasphemous. In one colour picture of Elvis he is dressed as Jesus and reveals his sacred heart as in a popular Roman Catholic image of Christ.

The Elvis story is frequently told as a parallel Gospel. "He was born in a house little bigger than a stable," fans relate, "and at the moment of his birth a strange blue light hovered over the place."

The account is given authenticity by Larry Geller, Elvis's hairdresser and spiritual adviser, who first heard about the strange light, he recalls, from Elvis's father Vernon. Larry's account has been much embroidered and the blue light is now identified with the star of Bethlehem and the whole night of Elvis's birth in a run-down shack in Tupelo has been given a mystical quality in narrative and song.

The Australian singer-songwriter Nick Cave's album *The Firstborn is Dead* shrouds the event in dark mystery. "The black rain came down, water

water everywhere. No bird can fly no fish can swim until the King is born in Tupelo!"

The Christ connection goes further than the story of his birth. George Klein was one of Elvis's close friends from school days. "Elvis really was something special. He wasn't just a normal human being. I don't want to be sacrilegious, but he was Jesus-like."

Another friend of Elvis has described how she was with him one evening and he began to glow as if he was being transfigured like Jesus.

Maia Shamayyim-Nartoomid saw Elvis perform on 36 occasions and believes she remains in mystical contact with him. "As a boy," she says, "Elvis would see shining beings who told him that he was blessed and sent to Earth for a special purpose. He came from the blue star in the system of Orion to bring a new message of love and peace to the world."

There is even a hint that Elvis was miraculously conceived, for at the moment of conception Vernon is said to have passed out and left his body. One internet gospel site quotes the words it claims were given to Vernon in a dream just after the conception. "Behold Vernon fruit of Jesse, stay with Gladys Love and remain her husband for in her womb is conceived the Holy Spirit of the rock that will break upon the world. And you shall call the child Elvis, which means all

LONESOME TONIGHT?: *(Top):* Worshippers in Pennsylvania. *(Bottom):* The Rev. Mort Farndu and Dr Karl N Edwards united in thier mission to bring Elvis to the galaxy.

wise because he is coming into the world to be proclaimed the King."

According to the Elvis Gospel version of his life, Elvis's death from an overdose of prescribed drugs in the bathroom at his home is given purpose. The suffering of the obese and junk-food guzzling singer is likened to the Passion of Christ. Shortly before his death Elvis's closest companions had written and published a damning account of Presley's life. Those companions in Elvis legend take on the role of Judas and thus Elvis, like Jesus, died in ignominy betrayed by his friends.

That he has been sighted since his death, it is said, is evidence not of a faked demise, but of a kind of resurrection.

There are tens of thousands of Elvis fans worldwide. Some enjoy his music and take their dedication no further. Others make shrines to Elvis in their homes and travel to Graceland on pilgrimage to attend the candle-lit vigil held every August on the anniversary of his death. In 1997 more than 30,000 fans filed silently past his grave in the memorial garden at the singer's Memphis mansion.

Every year hundreds of thousands of fans write messages on the Graceland wall. Some take the form of prayers to Elvis. And to give the Elvis following an extra religious dimension, the Elvis impersonators, or tribute singers, act as a kind of priesthood. The tribute concerts take a form similar to the Christian Mass with the Elvis look-a-like moving through the congregation handing out scarves and kisses like communion.

The Elvis impersonators also conduct weddings and the Elvis chapels in Memphis and Las Vegas get particularly busy on St Valentine's day and on Elvis's birthday in January each year.

One leading Elvis performer, David Moore, who gives shows at a hotel opposite Graceland on Elvis Presley Boulevard in Memphis, describes his work as a calling or ministry. "I have had people coming up to me who have said that it felt during my tribute as if Elvis was talking to them. I had one person who told me she had lost a son six months before and I had given her hope."

Inevitably the signs of the development of an Elvis religion has fascinated academics. Indeed, Elvisology, if that is the right word, is becoming a new university subject. The introduction to one American University course makes what must be the ultimate claim, that the best way to understand the start of Christianity in its early days is to study what has happened to Elvis over the last 20 years.

In the same way that early Christianity grew out of Judaism and the internal debates within that religion two thousand years ago, so an Elvis religion appears to be developing out of the Christian culture and heritage of late 20th-century Bible Belt America. And from there the message has reached the wider world. So much so that truly dedicated Elvis fans are now found in most European countries, in Japan and in Israel, where three of the world's great faiths have their holiest places. There is now a statue to Elvis in Israel which every Elvis fan going as a tourist to the Holy Land hopes to see.

How is it explained that Elvis Presley has become the focus of spirituality? He recorded a great deal of Gospel music and it is that which his most religious fans listen to most often. The feelings he expresses, whether spiritual or emotional, are easily accessible to people without a religious upbringing or theological education. He purveys fast food for the soul.

In his life Elvis was also himself fascinated by religion. With Larry Geller he studied New Age and esoteric writing and he often read the Bible. He was searching for an explanation for his astonishing worldly success.

The writer on religious affairs Karen Armstrong summed up the appeal of Elvis is this way on a BBC *Everyman* documentary in 1997.

"People are mythologising Elvis and are trying to express in conventional archetypical universal religious language what Elvis has meant for their inner lives, just as they did with Jesus, just as they did with Mohammed. People have somehow found the sacred in Elvis, strange as it may seem."

WHOLE LOTTA LOVIN': *(Top)*: The New Improved Testament. *(Middle)*: The 31 Commandments. *(Bottom)*: Elvis-vangelists.

INEPT CRIME

Crime doesn't pay, and, for this bunch of criminally inept felons, it didn't even work

THIEVES IN Ryton, Tyne and Wear, scaled a 6ft (1.8m) fence, dodged two Alsatian guard dogs and forced bolts and locks to get into Bob Hodgson's pigeon loft. They made off with 40 homing pigeons in three wicker baskets. Surprise, surprise – 24 hours later, all but eight of the birds had flown back to the loft. The remaining eight were fledglings who had probably not yet learned to fly.

SIDONIA WILLIAMS, a retired court clerk, wanted to open a charge account at a department store on New York's Fifth Avenue. Asked how she would pay, she reached into her duffel bag and presented a $1,000,000 bill. The police found 194 counterfeit or altered bills in her bag. Making money was her hobby, she said. To make the $1,000,000 bill, she pasted zeroes on a $1 bill and ran it off on a colour copier. Last May, federal magistrate Ronald Ellis tried to explain to Williams that the government did not make $1,000,000 bills and that it is illegal to make your own. Willams disagreed. "In this case it was legal, sir," she said.

ON 21 May, army private Daniel Bowden, 20, robbed his own federal credit union in Fort Belvoir, Virginia, of $4,759. Twelve days later, he was arrested when he returned and tried to deposit the loot in his personal account through the very bank teller he had held up. Bowden, who did not wear a mask, is a military police officer with training in handling bank robberies. He is also a suspect in the robbery of another northern Virginia bank on 12 May.

STEPHEN KING II tried to rob the Bank of America branch of Merced, California, in April by brandishing his uncovered finger and thumb and demanding money. The teller asked King to wait, then walked away. King got tired of waiting, so he crossed the street to another bank where he jumped over the counter and tried to get the key to a cash drawer. An employee grabbed the key and told him to get out. Police found him sitting in the bushes nearby.

A WEEK later, David Hindmarsh strolled into a bank in Fort Lauderdale, Florida, and informed a teller that he had a pipe bomb and wanted money. The teller said he had to wait – so he rejoined the queue. Twenty minutes later, he was given a bag containing $1,500, but outside the bank police and TV cameras were waiting for him, as the bank teller had given the alarm. Hindmarsh was arrested without a struggle. The 'bomb' was a lavatory roll.

AN ISRAELI thief who ransacked a house in Haifa agreed to a date with policewoman Yardena Rahamim when she rang him on the mobile phone he had stolen. Dressed to the nines and reeking of aftershave, the 22-year-old suspect drove to his nemesis in a car he had stolen in the break-in.

ROSIE LEE Hill called the police in Pensacola, Florida, in March and complained that she had been sold fake crack cocaine. An officer came round and was shown two 'rocks' which Lee said tasted like baking soda. The officer agreed, but found the stuff was real crack. Ms Hill, 35, was busted.

MEANWHILE IN Bayreuth, southern Germany, a man called a mobile telephone number, ordered 0.85lb (25g) of illegal amphetamines and arranged a meeting place for the handover. The only trouble was that the number had been given to him by the police during questioning last year. In the event, the customer got handcuffs rather than speed.

www.arttoday.com

SUSPICIOUSMINDS

MARK PILKINGTON dons the tin foil helmet to enter the labyrinthine world of the conspiracy theorists, returning with some of this year's best reasons to look over your shoulder.

I t wasn't just JFK's mind that was blown that fateful day in Dallas, 1963. The shooting shocked the world and, ever since, conspiracy theories have continued to enthral us with a morbid fascination. After all, everyone loves a mystery.

In the last year conspiracy thinking has seeped further and deeper into mainstream culture than ever before; from the very public utterings of Hillary Clinton and Mohammed Al Fayed to the latest adventures of Mulder and Scully, we've all had a glimpse, however brief, into the revolving hall of mirrors. But most of us only ever get to see the tip of the iceberg, the dead letterbox of the underground base. The deeper one gets the stranger things become, until the conspiracies appear so ridiculous they couldn't be true. Or could they..?

Wreckage: Workers recover parts of TWA 800

FLIGHTS OF FANCY?

IT'S BEEN over two years since the tragic and mysterious explosion of TWA 800 off Long Island. As yet investigators have failed to come up with a solution that incorporates all the elements described by witnesses, and conspiracies theorists are fast sealing up the gaps.

Suspicions were first aroused by the apparent entrapment of Long Island UFO investigator John Ford in June

1996. Ford was investigating what he believed were a series of UFO crashes between 1989 and 1995 in Long Island's Moriches Bay area where, a month after Ford's arrest, TWA 800 itself would come down. Ford has since been incarcerated in a psychiatric institution. His crime? Plotting to kill a local counsellor by spiking his toothpaste with radium – a process that would take over 40 years to become fatal. Although it's unlikely that UFOs were dropping from the skies over Long Island, it is possible that Ford stumbled across something he shouldn't have. Rumours of naval hardware testing and prototype aircraft flights are rife in the area and the TWA tragedy only seemed to confirm many half–formed suspicions.

Things are further complicated by bizarre and horrific tales emanating from deep inside an undersea mountain base at Montauk Point, a State Park on Long Island's northernmost tip, just 100 miles from New York City. This mountain must be pretty sizeable to house all the experiments said to go on there – psychotronic mind control testing on missing children, particle beams, weather control, interdimensional time travel and black hole simulators. According to researchers, Montauk is an extension of Project Pheonix, which included the legendary (and probably fictional) 1943 Philadelphia Experiment in battleship

invisibility. Although Phoenix is supposed to have shut down in 1983 after failing to raise enough public funding through the *Philadelphia Experiment* film, rumours of strange green flashes and gun-toting security thugs still plague the area today. It was, say certain conspiracists , a stray particle beam from the base which caused the demise of TWA 800.

MORE MAGIC BULLETS?

WHAT WOULD a year in conspiracies be without a good political assassination? The death of James Earl Ray saw new questions asked about the killing of Martin Luther King. Meanwhile in the Holy Land, a more recent murder was raising a few eyebrows.

Israeli UFO and conspiracy researcher Barry Chamish is convinced that then Prime Minister Yitzhak Rabin was killed on November 4th, 1995 in a political double bluff gone tragically wrong. The self–confessed assassin, Yigal Amir, was a mushy–minded patsy, the victim of a secret–service brainwashing plot to smear right–wing hardliners. So it looks like they messed that one up then.

As in all such shootings, there is a film. Taken by amateur cameraman Roni Kempler from a rooftop overlooking Rabin's high security motorcade, it apparently shows a very peculiar series of events.

BLANKS! BLANKS!: Security guards get it wrong in the Holy Land

As Rabin approaches an awaiting vehicle, his four trusted bodyguards appear to stall deliberately, giving Amir a clear shot at the PM. He fires twice. Instead of being hurled forwards by Amir's first shots, Rabin actually turns around, apparently unhurt, his clothing undamaged. At this point, claims Chamish, several witnesses heard an agent yell "Blanks, blanks. Not real," though this and the actual moment of impact are conspicuously absent from Kempler's film.

Next, bodyguard Yoram Rubin leaps to protect Rabin and Amir, still unchallenged, fires again at the PM. But Rabin remains apparently unaffected by the assault, despite, according to the official report, having landed a couple of hollow point 9mm bullets in his lungs and spleen. He enters his car without difficulty, leaving no blood on the pavement outside. So if Amir was firing blanks, how did Rabin die? Simple – there was a hit man in the car. A week after the murder Yoav Kuriel, a policeman assigned to protect Rabin, was found dead. Officials say he died of natural causes and his internal organs were removed for a transplant. However, an unnamed medical informant told Chamish that Kuriel's body had seven gunshot wounds in its chest. Could Kuriel have been Rabin's real killer?

MAD COWS AND MYSTERY CHOPPERS

CATTLE MUTILATIONS are one of the most bizarre and cherished mysteries of the late 20th century, but now researcher Ted Oliphant III thinks he may have stumbled upon the answer. Oliphant makes the connection between these mutilations and agencies unknown – perhaps the US Army, working in conjunction with disease control groups – monitoring the spread of Transmissible Spongiform Encephalopathies, i.e. BSE, throughout the US ranching industry.

Oliphant argues that to accurately assess the spread of the disease, the mutilators would need to find diseased and dying cows in their natural habitats. Locating them is easy – sick or dying cattle experience a sudden drop in hide temperature, so they just find the cold ones using stealth choppers equipped with infra-red night-vision equipment.

The next step is to incapacitate the animal – you don't want a half–tonne heifer kicking around while you're coring out its rectum. A curare-like poison does the trick, paralysing the animal and halting blood flow, making it easier to drain and operate without staining your slacks.

The removal of flesh and internal organs is the final part of the process, traditionally the jaw, tongue, digestive and reproductive organs. All essential for discovering how chemicals and toxins are ingested, absorbed and passed on to other members of the herd.

Mystery solved? Probably not – the mutilations have been around far longer than BSE has been a problem – but who's to say? The European BSE scare is justification enough for the secrecy surrounding these bizarre examinations, and can you imagine an America without McDonalds?

So perhaps the mutilations are for the best. Unless, of course, you're a cow.

STARLIGHT EXPRESS?

And before you leave smugly thinking that only other countries are plagued by such conspiracies, here's one a little closer to home – right under our very noses...

Britain and Ireland are in fact connected by a huge network of underground tunnels. What's more, a high speed military train service will get you from Downing Street to the underground facilities at Wiltshire's UFO mecca Rudloe Manor in just 20 minutes, complete with buffet car serving strawberry ice cream and royal jelly. According, that is, to an anonymous military source currently fearing for his safety. Others are more concerned for his sanity.

Meanwhile, a crack squadron of Blue Berets is in operation recovering crashed UFOs and hiding them deep under Salisbury Plain, where test flights of back-engineered black triangles are a regular occurrence. One squadron of troops was even witnessed being abducted by a blue beam fired from a mysterious craft in the area. There are also the usual dark tales of joint US/UK and ET bio-engineering experiments, implants, cattle, sheep and even human mutilations. Thankfully research by Kevin McClure and others has shown that these rumours are a load of old bunkers.

Well that's quite enough for one year, but remember; just because you're paranoid, it doesn't mean they're not out to get you.

STICKY FINGERS

A unique property which might well have appealed to budding fortean speculators was sold during the year: Britain's only working treacle mine. The mine, at Dunchidoeck, near Exeter, was included in the grounds of Dunchidoeck House, a stately home formerly owned by a larger-than-life local character named Charlie Winckworth. Winckworth died in 1997 after many years as self-appointed Managing Director of Dunchidoeck Treacle Mines Incorporated. The asking price for the property was £450,000; it was sold in early January after a few months on the market.

Although redolent of Ken Dodd's Knotty Ash Jam Buttie mines, "treacle mines" are apparently all too real. The name is generally thought to come from the archaic meaning of "trea-cle", an antidote against the bites of wild beasts – one early Bible is known as the "Treacle Bible" because it translates "balm" as "treacle". According to *Brewer's Dictionary of Phrase and Fable*, the word eventually came to be applied to one partic-

ular purportedly health-giving concoction, "Venice treacle, a blend of some sixty-four drugs in honey". Presumably, some medicinal sub-stance was once extracted from the mine, or the mine itself was thought to hold some medicinal property, similar to the Irish tradition of "healing wells".

Winckworth, perhaps inevitably, was more keen to play up the comedy potential of treacle mining. He was often pictured leaning on a "wadkin" (supposedly a special treacle barrel holding four gallons) at the mouth of the mine, pickaxe in hand and safety helmet securely on his head. Visitors to the estate would traditionally be shown the entrance to the mine, where a lone miner could often be seen hard at work; sadly, they were allowed to go no further, "in case they came to a sticky end."

Winckworth also concocted a lengthy and detailed history for the mine, full of bizarre "historical" details and groan-inducing puns. Treacle, it says, is the result of millennia-old sugar cane being com-pressed by rock, in much the same manner as oil is formed from other vegetable matter. Britain was once covered in treacle mines, but follow-ing a punitive tax introduced in 1781 (which gave us the term 'VAT', as tax on treacle was set at 42 shillings per vat), most were closed. The village of Dunchidoeck was occupied by the Roundheads under General Fairfax during the Civil War; the history notes that one local family bears the name of Fairfaxson, while another has traditionally always named their first son 'Oliver'. Current production is said to be some 700 wadkins, most of which is exported to North America. A pipkin (another unique treacle measure) is specially exported every year to the Kremlin.

This curious eccentricity even appears to have a precedent. The pre-vious occupants of Dunchidoeck House – a Pitman family – are thought to have had a hand in preparing another, earlier "history" of the mine, which listed in great detail how the treacle ore "is nowadays detected by its fluorescence under ultra-violet illumination. It is extracted by picks or blasting, is crushed, ground and extracted with various organic sol-vents, then concentrated by vacuum distillation." The resulting brew, the earlier history has it, is matured for up to 10 years in wooden vats, which gives Dunchidoeck treacle its "distinctive" flavour.

Although estate agents Strutt and Parker, who handled the sale, were unable to provide any fur-ther details, we understand that Dunchidoeck's trea-cle mine is, at least, to remain part of the grounds. Whether its history expands under the new owners remains to be seen; given current trends, the mine will no doubt be discovered to have been aligned to Sirius by its original builders.

www.arttoday.com

FATHER LIONEL'S TOP **10** MYSTERIES

The good Rev. Lionel Fanthorpe – easy riding, ballad bawling presenter of Fortean TV – spares a moment from tending the flock to tell us about his own favourite phenomena.

here's no such thing as bad beer – but some beer is undeniably better than others. In the same way there's no such thing as a fortean phenomenon that isn't intriguing, but some intrigue me more than others. Being objective about real ale – or real mysteries – isn't easy. Taste and flavour are personal, subjective experiences – and so are our responses to the various types of fortean unsolved mysteries. Some viewers prefer ghosts to giants, sea monsters to sliders and check-outs to chupacabras. It's that unmistakable fortean aroma of insolubility wafting across from any genuine mystery that draws me like a hungry lion to a limping zebra.

ALEX HOWE

❶ CHUPACABRAS

EL CHUPACABRAS is something with big teeth, an alimentary canal which incorporates an industrial vacuum cleaner, and the ability to strike, suck and vanish back invisibly into the jungle immediately afterwards. Eye witness accounts describe anything from a gerbil the size of a Shetland pony to a cross between a kangaroo and a crocodile. Theories range from an alien, a genetic engineering experiment that went badly wrong and escaped, a loose cannon on Darwin's *Beagle* or a very sick psychopath who likes dressing up in weird costumes and killing small animals with a suction pump. It's not just the blood which el chupacabras goes for: some victims have been found with their livers sucked out as well. And he/she doesn't confine his/her activities to Puerto Rico. Reports continue to come in from Mexico and most of Central and South America. There's a tough and enthusiastic local police chief named Aponté who's having a personal vendetta with whatever el chupacabras eventually turns out to be. I'd love to go down and help him: and I strongly suspect that whatever el chupacabras is made of will readily succumb to both barrels of a 10-guage magnum at close range — if it doesn't, I'll take him on hand-to-hand.

JOHN SIBBICK

❷ MIRACLE FISH

IN KANGAL, turkey there's a warm, shallow pool where the water has a remarkably high mineral content. The first miracle is that any fish can live in it at all. The second miracle is the symbiotic relationship which its hungry little denizens have with human beings. If you're unlucky enough to suffer from eczema, psoriasis or any similar skin problems, there's a fair chance that the Kangal surgeon fish can help to relieve the symptoms for you. The Kangal pool is like some kind of aquatic fortean NHS Centre. The staff have different skills and perform different functions: type one removes the damaged skin; type two cleans it up and type three seals it over.

www.arttoday.com

❸ TIME SLIPS

FROM THE philadelphia experiment in the States to the Roman mystery at Wroxham Broad in Norfolk, time-slips are among the most intriguing fortean experiences ever reported. The one we investigated on the show concerned two keen metal detecting friends from the Shrewsbury area. One night they'd gone out together as usual to an area called Boulder Field where they'd had some success on previous occasions. As they crossed the field on this particular evening they heard what sounded like the final furlong of the Grand National. It also sounded as if they were standing right in front of whoever, or whatever, was crossing Boulder Field like bats out of hell. One hallmark of a reliable eye-witness account is the honest admission that someone lost his cool when the fortean phenomenon arrived – and unashamedly ran like the devil. The men ran fast – in opposite directions – as what sounded like Roman cavalry thundered past them. They saw nothing, but the frightening noise of wildly galloping horses was unmistakable. They got together again, totally bewildered by their experience, and decided to head back over Boulder Field towards their car, their sandwiches and a flask of good hot coffee to steady their nerves. Halfway across the field they encountered a stockade wall which they knew could not possibly be there. It certainly hadn't been there when they'd started work. Frightened and mystified, they turned and followed the line of the stockade in the darkness. At last they reached a corner and turned again, this time in the direction of their car – from which the inexplicable stockade had temporarily separated them. At the first light of dawn they went back to examine the field. The unexplained stockade which had diverted them so effectively in the darkness had vanished: but their footprints hadn't. Their tracks showed exactly where the stockade had forced them to make a 90 degree diversion. When the two friends took some ancient metal finds from Boulder Field to an expert at Shrewsbury Museum, he said they were Roman cavalry harness fittings.

www.arttoday.com

❹ THE HAUNTED CAPRI

KEVIN CARLYON

ARK 666Y

IN EASTBOURNE near Beachy Head a cherished number plate dealer showed us a venerable Ford Capri with a fortean history and the sinister registration plate ARK 666Y. Having had it exorcised by a white witch, I added a gently persuasive exorcistic word of my own to anything unfriendly that might have been lurking in the upholstery: "Don't mess with me, Entity-Boy – I'm a Priest in the old Templar tradition. Try anything on me and I'll fry you!" Then I climbed in behind the wheel and drove the Capri around for an hour or so. I didn't get swept over Beachy Head, and I didn't get nobbled by any Eastbourne traffic wardens for parking it while we were filming. Prior to the exorcism, one of the old Capri's front wheels had inexplicably caught fire, and a friend of the owner was so startled by a strange apparition on the rear seat that she adamantly refused ever to enter the car again. Maybe that delicately refined and respectable Capri ghost wasn't anxious to take on a skinhead, Harley Davidson gorilla with neck muscles that strained against its eighteen-inch clerical collar.

ALEX HOWE

❺ WEEPING ELVIS

AN ENTHUSIASTIC Presley fan from Holland has a bust of Elvis in his collection of tasteful, high quality memorabilia. Every now and then water trickles unaccountably from the eyes as if it's weeping. Statues of saints have been alleged to do similar things, but when it comes to perspiring porcelain, this one's the king.

❻ GOBI DESERT DEATH WORM

IF YETIS roam the Himalayan peaks and Sasquatch prowl around the Canadian Rockies, what horrors unguessed-at might crawl below the sands of the Gobi Desert? The tough, local Mongolians are not only convinced of its physical existence, many of them believe that the Death Worm is a psychic phenomenon as well – a kind of Gobi Desert demon. If an electric eel can deliver a massive shock under water, there are no technical reasons why the Mongolian Death Worm can't deliver a few hundred volts on dry land. According to one or two survivors of encounters with the unfriendly brute, it produces a deadly toxin as well, which it spits malevolently at its victim. The only positive factor in the various accounts of the Death Worm's endearing little habits is that he, she, or it, keeps itself to itself in something akin to hibernation or suspended animation for ten months of the year, emerging with malicious enthusiasm to despatch the uninformed only in June and July. It's best to take your package holiday in Mongolia early or late season.

⑦ MERMAIDS

www.arttoday.com

MERMAIDS IN mythology, legend, song and story range from the sentimentalised hybrid beauty of Hans Christian Andersen's classic weepy to the ugly little mer-beast from the museum that we arranged to have autopsied on *Fortean TV*. Ours turned out to be a wooden replica that had in all probability been launched by a Polynesian fisherman as a votive offering to the sea-gods. But when Andersen, Disney and the piscine pathologists have all finished with her, the mermaid still clings tenaciously to the remains of her marine mystery like a first-time stripper clinging to her G-string. There is scientific speculation that the mermaid is just the grotesque old dugong (sea-cow), seen from a great distance by homesick sailors in need of better telescopes. Some sightings can undoubtedly be explained that way – but I strongly suspect that others can't. What if we try linking mermaid reports with the equally persistent myths and legends of intelligent, aquatic aliens, modified, fish-tailed survivors of Atlantis or Lemuria, and sinister tales of the magical, oceanic Quinotaurs and Tritons which seem to have had a predilection for human females – as was the case with King Merovee's mum? She may not look exactly like the romantic Victorian artists' version of her – but in a universe full of infinite possibilities, something more like a Disney mermaid than a dugong may swim into Cardiff Bay one moonlit night asking for political asylum and a towel.

⑧ DOC SHIELS AND MORGWAR

THAT LOVEABLE, outgoing, larger than life character, Tony "Doc" Shiels, did his best to conjure up Morgawr the Cornish Sea Monster for us. Morgawr's the Falmouth Bay equivalent of Nessie. Maybe this time we just didn't have enough beautiful, naked and nubile young witches available to lure the beast from the deep. But just because Morgawr didn't oblige us this time doesn't mean it's not lurking out there somewhere under the Falmouth waves. The jury's still out on whether sea and lake monsters exist, but remembering the big surprise the coelacanth gave the experts after a ten million year absence, I'm inclined to vote "Yes".

⑨ YETI AND SASQUATCH

WHEN ALL the evidence has been weighed, the reports read, the film footage and photographs analysed, the strong probability remains that some weird, unknown cryptozoological species lurks high in the Canadian Rockies and the Himalayas. If we ever win the big rollover lottery prize, my wife Patricia and I are off to the Rockies and the Himalayas with a properly equipped expedition, camera crew and sound team. I'm certain we'll bring back one of the most exciting documentaries ever made.

⑩ THE DOLPHIN MAN FROM CUBA

HOLDING YOUR breath for two minutes is a commendable achievement. Japanese pearl-divers and a few professional stunt-artists can manage a little bit longer. Eight minutes puts you in the dolphin class – and that's exactly what Francisco Ferreras can do. This amazingly powerful Cuban diver and underwater swimmer can slow his heartrate down to seven beats per minute, and dive to nearly 450 ft (137m) with no protective apparatus. Most normal human beings — however tough – would probably be crushed to death at just over 300 ft (91m). Not surprisingly, Francisco holds 27 world records for free-diving. So how does this unique Cuban survive what would almost certainly kill most of us? The secret seems to lie in the unusual way in which his powerful body responds to external pressure: instead of simply caving in, it somehow reinforces his lungs with bodily fluids. It's easy enough to crush an empty beer can – but try crushing a full one! As the increasing external water pressure threatens to collapse his chest while he dives ever deeper, Francisco's lungs resist it by increasing their internal pressure with natural fluid to match it. His incredibly slow heart beats are the result of years of yoga studies in India and China. Apart from being a mystery in his own right, Francisco raises intriguing questions about the evolutionary links between human beings and dolphins. Maybe *Homo sapiens* didn't so much swing down from the trees as pop up out of the sea?

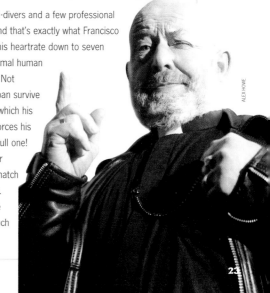

ALEX HOWE

STUPID AND
WEIRD BEHAVIOUR

Whenever *Fortean Times'* editors come together to plough through the thousands of clippings we get each month, the stories that get read out as we go along tend not to be of lake monsters, or crop circles, or UFOs, but of strange human behaviour. Sometimes it seems that there is nothing so odd or stupid that somebody hasn't done it or had it done to them.

ED TRAQUINO

ALFONSO NIÑO, 75, a retired Navy pilot from Nipoma, California, is listed in the telephone directory as Al Niño. Since the cataclysmic storms which lashed America at the start of 1998, he has had more than 100 calls a day from people who believe that he is the "El Niño" which caused them. One caller blamed him for his daughter's losing her virginity because she was unable to get home after a storm had blocked the road and she had had to spend the night in the car with her boyfriend.

CHONG KIM Lee, a 61-year-old chef, was jailed for 15 years for trying to have sex with an elephant. He was caught naked from the waist down, standing on a box behind the animal. The father of five claimed that the elephant was the reincarnation of his wife Wey. She had died 28 years ago, shortly before her 29th birthday. Chong told the court in Phuket, Thailand: "I recognised her immediately because of the naughty glint in her eye."

IN FEBRUARY, Adolph Lu Hitler was tipped to hold on to his seat in elections in Meghalaya, a state in north-east India, despite a strong challenge from Churchill Lyngdoh. A week later, Spanish police stepped up their hunt for a Peruvian highwayman called Hitler Escalante, whose gang rob tourists on the Costa Brava motorway near Barcelona. And in March, Adolf Hitler Kwok Kin-Wing lost his appeal against molesting a 17-year-old schoolgirl in Hong Kong.

MARK GALLAGHER of Kilburn, London, made a 45-minute tape of a vacuum cleaner and left it playing at full volume every morning at 7.00am when he went to work. His upstairs neighbour endured months of misery before local noise-

pollution inspectors were called in. Gallagher was fined £100 and ordered to pay £1,250 costs.

A PRISON in Lima, Peru, got prisoners to make new uniforms for guards as part of a cost-cutting exercise, but 28 inmates made uniforms for themselves and strolled past unwitting guards to freedom.

POLICE WERE called to a house in Polegate, Sussex, after the owner claimed that someone had broken in and watched a video. Nothing was taken and there was no sign of a forced entry, but the video – which didn't belong to the home owner – had been left in the machine. Unfortunately, we don't know what was on the tape.

PRIVATE DETECTIVES followed a man from Notton, South Yorkshire, for four years in an attempt to prove that an accident had not left him as severely injured as he claimed. They secretly filmed him living an apparently normal life. Only when the film was sent to William Hood's solicitors was it discovered that they had been following his neighbour, Peter Arnott, by mistake. Hood won his claim for damages and Arnott was considering suing for invasion of privacy.

A MYSTERY man who claimed to be working for the local council took a chainsaw to an entire wood of 200 sycamores and alders along the A167 Great North Road near Durham City – and then just left them lying there. Police were stumped as to a motive. "Before he arrived, there was an avenue of 15-year-old trees which had grown to a height of about 20ft (6m) with trunks about 10in (25cm) thick," said council spokesman Andrew Jackson, "now there is nothing left."

MEDICAL BAG

At *Fortean Times* we never cease to be amazed by the curiosities thrown up by the world of medicine. Here's a short selection of some of our favourites.

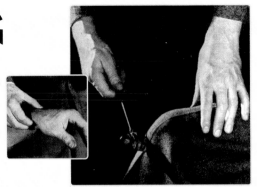

Both images: www.arttoday.com

POCKET MONSTERS

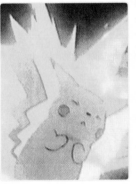

At the end of last year, 685 people, mainly children, were taken to hospitals across Japan after watching *Pokemon*, a cartoon on TV Tokyo based on the *Pocket Monsters* computer game. More than 48 hours after the broadcast, 218 people, aged from three upwards, including a man of 58, were still in hospital with epilepsy-like seizures, and two were still there a week later. A five-year-old girl from Osaka had trouble breathing and was said to be in a serious condition. It is estimated that 4.15 million households nationwide were tuned in to the broadcast.

The trouble started with a scene, 20 minutes into the programme, in which a 'vaccine bomb' explodes in an attempt to kill a computer virus – or possibly where rat-like Pikachu, the main character, creates lightning to counter missiles (accounts differ). The screen was filled by a bright red explosion and strobe lights, followed by a white flash and the eyes of Pikachu, flashing red.

The five second sequence provoked fits, vomiting of blood, eye irritation and breathing difficulties. Yet more children were afflicted later in the evening when some news programmes replayed the scene and other children watched pre-recorded videos of the half-hour show. A survey by school officials found that at least 7,000 children reported feeling ill. Many said their memory of the show had been wiped clean.

TV Tokyo and Shogakkan, *Pokemon*'s production company, were astonished that animation techniques used hundreds of times before could provoke such a reaction. They cancelled further broadcasts and asked outside experts to investigate. Last March, four children were hospitalised after watching a different cartoon, but no causal relationship was discovered. The *Pokemon* cartoon had been running on TV Tokyo and its 37 network stations since last April and had the highest ratings in the Tokyo region for its 6.30pm slot.

The fast-paced cartoons produced by Japan's multi-billion-dollar animation industry require intense concentration and children in the country's cramped homes tend to watch them on increasingly large screens from less than 3ft (1m) away. About 7.5 million copies of Nintendo's black-and-white *Pocket Monsters* role-playing computer game have been sold in less than two years, making it the best seller.

British TV programmes and video games are tightly regulated to ensure they do not trigger fits in the 17,000 people in Britain believed to suffer from photosensitive epilepsy.

STRANGE TUSCAN SNOOZE

IN THE early months of 1998, thirteen apparently healthy residents of the Tuscan village of Camigliano fell into a prolonged comatose sleep for periods of between 15 and 36 hours. Most of the – mainly elderly – victims lived in cottages near a garden in the village, while the rest use the garden regularly while visiting relatives. On waking, the victims had no memory of what happened or of any dreams, and no symptoms of any identifiable illness. For a while, residents suggested that the village was "bewitched, like in a fairy tale". However, a married couple in the village went on trial in September, charged with poisoning the victims.

The attacks first came to light in April when an 80-year-old woman was taken to hospital in Lucca in an apparent coma. Doctors carried out a range of tests without finding anything wrong. She woke up and was sent home. Another victim fell asleep suddenly for prolonged periods ten times in a row. The victims included two elderly sisters, a couple in their fifties visiting their mother and a woman of 51. One woman of 49 fell asleep while driving. She crashed into a wall, but escaped with minor injuries. When she woke up, she was unable to recall a thing.

Those who have witnessed the results of the "mystery illness" claim that people suffering from it are often able to talk coherently when they otherwise seem to be asleep, and in some cases can even get up and eat. Doctors initially described the outbreak as "hypersomnia with transitory global amnesia", but were at a loss to explain it.

SLEEPING SLAVES

IN LATE September, Mariano and Claudia Rocchi, both 45, appeared in court, accused of lacing the drinks and food of the village's inhabitants with a sedative. The prosecution alleged that they hoped that their victims would employ them to run errands and help out around the house.

www.arttoday.com

STRANGE

MARK TWAIN said that nothing is certain in life except for death and taxes. What he seemed not to know is that sometimes the Grim Reaper appears in the oddest guises, as this bumper bundle of demented demises shows.

KOBAL

☠ A 66-YEAR-OLD Croatian woman was killed by her grandson's 80lb (36kg) Staffordshire terrier whose life she had spared two years earlier. Katarina Paunovic of Novska, southeast of Zagreb, was sitting on her porch on 8 June when the four-year-old pet went for her neck, severing an artery. Her grandson had wanted to put the animal down when it bit him, but she successfully pleaded for its life.

☠ HASHIEM ZAYED, 59, a short-order cook, and waitress Helen Menicou, 47, had worked together at the Pine Crest Diner in San Francisco for 22 fractious years. On 23 July she publicly scolded him for making poached eggs for a customer when it was not on the menu. This was the last straw: the next day he came to work and shot her dead.

☠ ANTON CRUDSCH was so upset when councillors were ordered to bring their own lavatory paper to meetings in Kalofer, Bulgaria, that he went home for his shotgun and shot dead mayor Simeon Krasnich.

☠ AWERTO ALVADOROS, 34, exploded and died as surgeons in Guayaquil, Ecuador, used a scalpel to open him up. Heat from the instrument ignited methane in his gut, creating a ball of flame. Operating staff suffered minor injuries and shock.

☠ WHEN HIS owner collapsed with a coronary in Bonn, Otto the Rottweiler defended him against paramedics for 12 minutes. By the time they got Otto to move, the 68-year-old was dead. Still, it's the thought that counts.

DEATHS

☠ A BRITISH actor hanged himself on 17 August while playing Judas during an open-air performance of Jesus Christ Superstar in front of an audience of 600 holiday makers at a Greek hotel. Tony Wheeler, 26, failed to attach the rope to a hook on his back designed to support his weight. He remained hanging above a small rise at the dimly-lit side of the stage for about six minutes before the actors and audience realised that his initial spasms weren't part of his performance.

☠ A 32-YEAR-OLD man died on 9 April when a camp site lavatory exploded as he tried to light a cigarette, blasting him through a closed window. Police in Montabaur, south of Bonn, said the explosion appeared to have been caused by leaking gas from the septic tank or a defective natural gas pipe.

☠ EGYPTIAN FARM worker Susu Bora Mohammad, 22, accidentally swallowed some ants when she took a swig of water. She went home and swallowed some insecticide to kill the ants, but suffered diarrhoea and convulsions and died immediately after being taken to hospital in the Qena district of Cairo.

☠ A WOMAN driver in Denver, Colorado, choked to death when she swallowed her lipstick. Police say she was doing her make-up when she braked suddenly.

☠ THIERRY SIGAUD, 31, shot and killed his mother on 6 September after she gave him a haircut he did not like, in preparation for a local carnival in Nevers, France. His father tried to intervene and was also shot dead.

☠ STEFAN ROSENGREN, 29, a travel writer, leapt to his death from the Clifton Suspension Bridge in Bristol after getting depressed about the miserable summer. He had returned home in May after four years in south-east Asia. "The rain in June got to him," his brother, Gudmend, told the inquest in Bristol.

☠ SIEK PHAN, 62, a Vietnamese woman from the Cambodian province of Kompong Speu, was cutting firewood when her husband, Nou Meas, 65, sneaked up and tickled her. She instinctively threw her axe, killing him instantly. When she turned round, she found she had nearly decapitated him. "I hate being tickled," she told the authorities.

☠ CHILDREN'S ENTERTAINER Marlon Pistol was killed when a 20ft (6m) balloon elephant used in his act inflated in the back of his car on a California highway.

☠ TWO BROTHERS were told by community elders in Delhi to hold their breath underwater as a way of settling a family argument – the one who lasted longer would win. Both drowned.

☠ STAG PARTY friends were curious when a stripper failed to jump out of a huge cake in Cosenza, Italy. On opening it, they found her dead inside. Gina Lalapola, 23, had suffocated after waiting for an hour inside the sealed cake.

☠ FELIPE ORTIZ, 48, fishing in Colombia, cast a line into the teeth of a gale and suffocated when the bated hook blew back into his throat. Efforts to save him by slapping his back failed.

☠ A GERMAN couple in their 50s took their old car to a scrapyard. They parked, completed the paperwork, but got back in the car to shelter from a sudden squall of rain. "The driver of the crane was told to process their car", said a police investigator. "He did so without realising that the couple were sitting inside again." The car was grabbed by the crane's steel claws and dropped in the crusher, which normally reduces cars to a small cube. It was stopped when the crane driver heard the woman's screams, but it was too late to save her husband.

☠ THE CHIEF accountant from the failed Japanese brokerage Yamaichi Securities Co. worked without a break for 14 days from a week before the crash (Japan's largest post-war failure) and did not leave the office during that period. The 38-year-old man finally went home in Tokyo on 27 November and was found dead in bed the next morning. Verdict: fatigue.

☠ GARY HARMON, 47, died on 10 September 1997, after a nine-day stay in St Joseph Mercy-Oakland Hospital in Pontiac, Michigan, where he was being treated for asthma and emphysema. He complained about something being stuck in his throat which he couldn't cough up. He was rushed back to hospital, but died two hours later, having choked on a latex surgical glove.

There are hundreds more tales of odd departures in The Fortean Times Book Of More Strange Deaths.

MORE**STRANGE**DEATHS

☠ **FOURTEEN PATIENTS**, including four newborn babies in incubators, died after a rat gnawed through the wiring of Catarino Rivas hospital in San Pedro Sula, northern Honduras, cutting off electricity. Six died when the power was cut to their life-support machines. The short circuit killed the rat.

☠ **VERNON SUCKERLOC**, 65, from Birmingham, Alabama, had collected his toenails for 55 years and had stored four tons of old clippings in his attic. One night, he was having his bath when the ceiling collapsed, showering him with old toenails and killing him instantly. His wife seemed unsympathetic. "He only married me because I'm a trained pedicurist," said Sally-Anne Suckerlog. We're not sure we believe a word of this.

☠ **ANDREW THORNTON**, 37, received a fatal shock as he turned on the shower at his home in Banbury, Oxfordshire, last July. A small screw used to tighten a loose floorboard on the landing outside the bathroom had penetrated wiring for the shower and caused a short circuit.

☠ **A ROMANIAN** woman, Florica Ifimie, hanged herself before her wedding because she could not agree with her bridegroom over the menu for the wedding feast.

☠ **DETECTIVE-SERGEANT DANIEL** Edwards, 40, was found on 30 August trapped between a tree and his patrol car on a road between Muizenberg and Fish Hoek, near Cape Town in South Africa. Captain Jacques Wiese said it appeared Sgt Edwards parked his vehicle on a slope when he went to relieve himself. The vehicle then rolled down the embankment and crushed him.

☠ **MAXINE ANN** Keccerreis, 79, died in Allegan, Michigan, while trying to exercise her dog and mow the lawn at the same time. She drowned in a pond after becoming entangled in the dog chain attached to her riding mower. She apparently tried to back up when the chain and mower snagged, and fell into the water with the dog, which also drowned.

☠ **CAROL WILLIAMS**, 54, of Townhill, Swansea, suffocated when she fell face-down into her dog's bowl and the bowl's rim pressed against her neck. The inquest heard she was three times over the drink-drive limit.

☠ **A SERB** man was bitten to death by a badger he was hunting when the animal ripped out a piece of flesh from his thigh and severed a vein.

☠ **PROSPERO CAPELLAR** Barrios, 46, a Venezuelan ice cream seller, was killed on 16 September when a cast-iron lamp post crashed down on the spot where he had worked for more than 14 years. Thieves had removed the lamp post's retaining screws. Barrios died of head wounds in the colonial centre of Caracas before medical help could arrive.

☠ **A RETIRED** miner, who never had an accident underground, died when a load of coal buried him in his own backyard in the former mining village of Nelson in Glamorgan. Tom Gray, 86, was getting fuel from his bunker when a wall collapsed.

☠ **IN AN** apparent case of ostension (folklore becoming actual news), wealthy Charles Felder, 71, died after his cleaner, 47-year-old Pauline Jassey, unplugged his life support machine to use the vacuum cleaner in his bedroom in Dallas, Texas.

☠ **A ROW** between rival collectors of bat excrement – a valuable resource used in organic fertiliser – left five dead and two seriously injured after a home-made grenade was tossed into the mouth of a bat cave in the Pak Chong district of Nakhon Ratchasima province in Thailand on 2 April. A survivor told police the group was leaving the cave with seven sacks-full when the explosion ripped through them. A rival gang of dungmen was suspected.

☠ **A 27-YEAR-OLD** French woman driving near Marseilles on 5 April killed a cyclist and injured another. She was distracted by her Tamagotchi virtual pet, attached to her car key ring, which started to send out distress signals. She asked a companion in the car to attend to the electronic ovoid, but in the confusion she failed to see a group of cyclists on the road ahead and slammed into the back of them.

☠ **PATRICIA NOSIGLIA**, 22, died in May after she picked up her phone receiver in Buenos Aires, Argentina and received a 13,000 volt shock that knocked her to the floor. Police said the shock was caused by an electric cable that crossed the telephone line running from the street to the house.

☠ **LARRY SLUSHER**, 47, from Arjay, Kentucky, asked his best friend to shoot a beer can off the top of his head. The friend obliged, aimed his .22 calibre semi-automatic at the can, but missed and shot Slusher in the head. He died in Knoxville two days later. Silas Caldwell, 47, also from Arjay, was, rather unfairly we feel, charged with murder.

☠ **WERNER SHENKE** bit off another man's ear in a bar room brawl in Bremen, Germany – and then choked to death on it.

KOBAL

LIFE AFTER I4O

Who wants to live forever? Here's the cream of the crop of oldies but goodies who have given it their best shot.

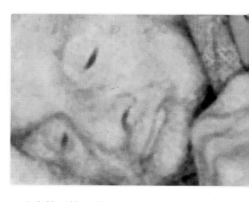

ALI MOHAMMED HUSSEIN (135 yrs)

Hussein (above), of Qinieh in northern Lebanon, has an identity document stating that he was born in 1862. Like all official records in Lebanon, the birth date is based on the country's only complete census, taken under French rule in 1932. Hussein, a former charcoal burner, can barely hear or see and his speech is virtually unintelligible, but he still gets around with the aid of a stick. He subsists on milk, green vegetables – and 60 cigarettes a day. He sings salacious songs for visitors in a low, croaking voice, encouraged by his wife, Amsha, who says she is thought to be between 80 and 90 years old.

MARIE-LOUISE MEILLEUR (II7 yrs 229 days)

Meilleur (right), was born Marie-Louise Febronie Chasse on 29 August 1880 in Kamouraska, 95 miles (153km) east of Quebec City. She had the edge over other claimants because the civil registries in Roman Catholic Quebec were meticulously maintained. Her family were able to provide her birth certificate, a census form from 1881, when she was eight months old, baptism papers and her two marriage licences. Mme Meilleur rolled her own cigarettes and smoked until she was in her nineties, but never touched alcohol or meat. Her secret of longevity was manual work and prayer. She had 12 children by her two husbands, 85 grandchildren, 80 great-grandchildren, 57 great-great-grandchildren and four great-great-great-grandchildren. When told she was the oldest person in Canada, she said: "Poor Canada". She died on 16 April 1998 in the Nipissing Manor Nursing Care Centre in Corbeil, Ontario, originally built in the 1930s as a nursery/theme park for the Dionne quintuplets, the world's first quins to survive infancy. Felicie Cormier, allegedly a year older than Mme Meilleur but with no birth certificate to prove it, died earlier the same day in Crowley, Louisiana.

BIR NARAYAN CHAUDHARI (I4I yrs, 5 months?)

In February, it was reported that Chaudhari, from the Nepalese village of Khanar near Biratnagar, was born in November 1856, although this was undocumented. He was teetotal, smoked a pipe and had never been to hospital. He lived on grapes, rice, pork, vegetables, yoghurt and water, and took four-hour catnaps every day. Every time his hair fell out, it grew back, sometimes white, sometimes black. He had also had four sets of teeth. He left his village twice, the first time about 80 years ago and the second in 1997, when he was taken to see the king in Kathmandu to be

granted citizenship and to receive an extraordinary service medal. He died on 20 April 1998. He was survived by four grandchildren, 16 great-grandchildren and four great-great-grandchildren, descendants of his son, Sobbalal, who died 10 years ago aged 85.

MARIE DO CARMO GERONIMO (I27+)

Ever since the 4 August 1997 death of Marie Calment, listed in *The Guinness Book of Records* as the world's oldest person (aged 122 years and 164 days), the race has been on for the longevity laurels. One rival during Calment's lifetime was the tiny ex-slave Maria Geronimo, 4ft 1in (1.2m) tall, who had an audience with the Pope in October 1997 during his visit to Brazil. Her age is not recognised by the international edition of *Guinness,* but the Brazilian edition accepts the validity of her baptismal certificate, which states that she was born on 5 March 1871. "My secret in life is this – to sing," she said.

CHRISTIAN MORTENSEN (II5 yrs 252 days)

For a while, *Guinness* bestowed the title of world's oldest person on Mortensen, a cigar-puffing Dane living in San Rafael, California. Impeccable birth records in Skaarup, Denmark, show the birth of Thomas Peter Thorvald Kristian Ferdinand Mortensen on 16 August 1882. He appeared on the 1901 Danish census and sailed for the United States in 1903. He had lived in 26 states and worked as a tailor, cowboy, boat builder, horse-and-buggy milkman and streetcar repair man. He died on 25 April 1998.

THE **DI** FILES

For many the death of Diana has been as perplexing a mystery as her life. IAN SIMMONS casts a doleful eye over some of the more unlikely stories surrounding her last hours.

O n the morning of 1 September 1997 I got up early in order to leave for a course I was attending, and on going downstairs, found our Lithuanian lodger in a state of distress. I asked her what was wrong. She said "Your Diana, she is dead in Paris." and I replied "Who shot her?" "It was a car accident - but political I think" was her reply.

We were not alone that morning, reputedly the first allegation of a conspiracy hit an Internet newsgroup six minutes after Diana's death was announced, and inevitably it did not stop there. In the Middle East at least six pamphlets alleging conspiracies surfaced within 48 hours, and by the Wednesday the alt.conspiracy.princess-diana newsgroup was up and receiving heavy traffic. Diana was proving to be as fertile a ground for conspiracy paranoia as JFK had been, without even the certainty that anyone had killed her – at least with JFK someone without a doubt had pulled a trigger (or triggers). The Diana conspiracy advocates have included some influential and well-placed individuals as well. Most prominent among these is Dodi's father, Mohammed Al-Fayed, who has funded his own extensive investigation and provided regular updates on his "evidence" via the *Daily Mirror* front page. Some more uncharitable pundits have suggested this is, however, merely an attempt to shift attention from security failures in his own organisation which led to the accident.

The lack of certainty as to whether the death of Diana was the result of a conspiracy or a cock-up led to intense scrutiny of the circumstances of her death. As it turned out, there was no shortage of factoids which could imply assassination, far too many to detail here.

These led to conspiracy theories which take two paths. The first involves how it was done, the second who did it and why. Most of the who and why theories use broadly the same how scenario. Driver Henri Paul may have been a "Manchurian Candidate" programmed assassin, or had been dosed with slow release alcohol capsules so he became intoxicated on the road. Strange photographers seen in the crowd were assassins who then used powerful bikes to pursue the car, leaving the real photographers behind. They herded the car in the direction they wanted, towards the Pont de l'Alma tunnel, cutting British secretary Brenda Wells off in the process, forcing her car to enter the

tunnel from a slip road. Once in the tunnel, they were joined by another car and carried out the assassination. Here, they may have used a powerful flash device disguised as a camera to disorient the driver or trigger his conditioning. Next one of the motorcyclists pulled ahead to spray the road with a chemical slick, after which the assassin's car sideswiped Diana's Mercedes to make it skid, or a remote-control device implanted when the Merc was stolen was used to over-ride the controls and run the car into the 13th pillar, or possibly a bomb was detonated somewhere on or in the vehicle, maybe a limpet mine placed by one of the bikers. After the impact a "fireman" seen reaching into the car before emergency services arrived – in fact one of the bikers – injects Paul with alcohol and/or Di with poison.

With the collusion of French officials the video tapes recording traffic along the car's route are removed, medical aid is slow to arrive and interference

a remote control device implanted when the Merc was stolen

afterwards ensures her death, then the tunnel is prematurely re-opened to cover forensic evidence and the investigation is purely cosmetic, covering up the truth.

If that could be the how, what about the who and why? In this opinions diverge far more widely.

MANGLED: The crumpled wreckage.

There are three main theories, with others launching off into increasingly baroque realms. The most publicly proclaimed one supported by Al-Fayed is what could be termed the Royal Theory. In this, the Royals or some part of the establishment horrified by Diana's engagement to a Moslem (though their engagement was never proven to be true) and embarrassed by her dabbling in politics over landmines etc. decided to eradicate her. A second widely-aired scenario accused arms dealers, anxious that Diana's campaign against mines would

ON THE WALL: Scrawled comments in France.

damage business, of rubbing her out. Specific culprits named were UK arms interests, the US military-industrial complex, and even the Chinese government, who are major mine exporters. The third one which appeared around the time of the death was the Escape theory, in which the whole thing was a fake to get Di out of the public eye, carried out with official French collusion so she and Dodi could live in blissful anonymity together.

While these three appeared relatively rapidly, more imaginative ideas emerged in the months following. Mossad were suggested as culprits, because Israel could have feared that if Di married a Moslem she would be influenced by Arab opinion and use her position to rally world support against Israel. Then there was the idea that the assassination was not aimed at Di at all, but at Dodi, derived from his involvement in arms deals through his uncle Adnan Khashoggi. He had offended one of his middle eastern connections who wiped him out with Di beside him as a warning to other potential transgressors. Or possibly it was drug related. Lyndon LaRouche, a leading American right-winger, and his followers claim the Royals head the world drug trade. If this is so, Di could have been killed because she had left the family knowing their

secrets and by joining up with the Al-Fayeds was allying herself with another gang, so had to be removed.

From here on in, things get weirder. According to pseudonymous internet correspondent "Ru Mills", it was all down to the New World Order planned by the Bilderberg group of international politicians. In this scenario, the present royals are impostors, but the true British royal lineage from the Stuarts carries on through the Spencers, and two factions, the New World Order, and Europe's true nobility, vied for control of her, as well as with internal factions in each camp. The NWO lot wanted to eliminate Hillary Clinton and have Di marry Bill, moving to the US and making Harry a US citizen so he could become a senator. With his brother on the British throne, whoever controlled them controlled the world. However Di refused to go along with this and was killed by MI6 as a result. Nonetheless, factions within MI6 opposed her death but, powerless to prevent it, ensured that it happened at Pont de l'Alma, sending a sign to the perpetrators and creating a "Saint Diana". The bridge was once a pagan sacrificial site, and in the time of the Merovingian kings (500-751AD), who some believe are descendents of Jesus, it was supposedly a place of King sacrifice, where a Royal victim was guaranteed a seat on God's right hand if they died there. With the help of holographic technology, visions of Diana would be then be produced worldwide, generating a Diana cult in which her sons would be akin to "living Jesus Christs", and whoever controlled them controlled the world. On the other hand, florid evangelist Texe Marrs saw the whole thing as a signifier of the End Time, with Diana as the Whore of Babylon

and her sons as likely antichrists.

Once we enter the occult conspiracy territory, things get very weird indeed, as a text mailed anonymously to Paranoia magazine revealed. Asserting that Queen Elizabeth is head of a family of Satanists it pointed out that 31 August was a significant date in the occult calendar, and that Diana had been groomed from childhood for her role as ritual sacrifice, implicating Tony Blair, Rupert Murdoch, Bill Clinton and others in this cult and highlighting links between the Spencers and the Ripper murders.

But the strangest allegations must be those I received by email from "Luther Blissett" in response to posting on Di conspiracy site . This was presumably not the footballer, but possibly an Italian Anarchist (there is a group who use it as a collective name) aligned with the London Psychogeographical Association, or someone pretending to be him. Psychogeography is the political manipulation of earth power using magic rituals and ley lines, and in this theory Diana was again a ritual sacrifice, but with a specific purpose. It was intended to realign the Omphalos - the psychic navel - of the British Empire for renewed world domination in the next millennium. To do this, Di's death was to act as a focus for manipulating the national psyche during the period of mourning. Diana was symbolically given the sacrificial role when she exchanged a "kiss of peace" with Prince Charles during VE Day

There is no smoking gun, just circumstantial evidence

celebrations in 1995 - as heir to the throne he would normally have been the victim, but as we have a Queen, the sacrifice had to be female, so he passed the role on in this way. Prior to that event, the Queen performed a ritual in Hyde Park with 59 heads of state symbolically placing England at the centre of the world. They wrote their names on olive leaves and attached them to the border of a circular map of the world derived from the idea of the "Land-hemisphere", portraying the landmasses of the earth in a single hemisphere with Britain at the centre. This laid out her intentions and the leaders' accession to this.

The Omphalos of the original British Empire was conjured into being on the Isle of Dogs by Dr John Dee, accompanied by Christopher Marlowe, on one of Britain's primary ley lines, gaining control of the current in a spot now marked by a replica hill fort in Mudchute park. A psychic backlash from this led to Marlowe's death in a Deptford pub brawl. Later, an attempt in the early 90's to seize the ley by British National Party occultists caused singer Ian Stewart, of Nazi band Skrewdriver to spontaneously combust at the wheel of his car when the establishment occultists retaliated. The Omphalos, however, was enfeebled after 400 years and needs renewal, so Diana was sacrificed in Merovingian ground and buried on an Island at Althorp - the Omphalos must be on an island or peninsula surrounded, or nearly so, by water. This is further up the same ley line as the original and almost in the centre of England. The Omphalos now focused on the burial

site, secured by a ritual carried out on the island during the funeral when Diana was laid to rest with the press and public excluded. Interestingly, a former Althorp retainer has complained that the island was traditionally the burial place of the Spencer dogs, so the Omphalos would seem to have moved from one isle of dogs to another, although what significance this has I'm not sure, but there has been a suggestion that this is connected with the Goddess Diana. As the goddess of the hunt, it would be appropriate for her to be surrounded by dogs.

Further, perhaps more frivolous, theories suggest Elton John did it to boost his career, or that florists did it to boost profits, although most of the theories I've outlined above present no better evidence than these do.

Do I think Diana was assassinated now ? Well, no. There is no smoking gun, just circumstantial evidence, and much of the theorising seems to derive from the belief that celebrities are not as others, that someone so famous can't die due to a stupid mistake - there has to be a reason. But it is not true, fame does not grant lives extra meaning, and the great can die just as pointlessly as the rest of us. What is certain though, is that the nexus of mangled wreckage, celebrity and beauty, so clearly articulated by JG Ballard in *Crash* will ensure Diana a vivid immortality, and the conspiracy theories will live on with her.

www.arttoday.com

As the goddess of the hunt, it would be appropriate for her to be surrounded by dogs.

LIFE THROUGH A LENSE: Diana and press photographers.

AP

STRANGE USA

ALASKA

A gunman who held up 21 people and forced them to whistle *Hail, Hail, The Gang's All Here* was being hunted in Alaska. He had never hurt anyone or stolen any property.

ISSAQUAH

A 43-year-old man was coaxed out of his home by police in Issaquah, Washington, after he pulled a gun on his personal computer and shot it, apparently in frustration. "We don't know if it wouldn't boot up, or what," said Sgt Keith Moon(!). The computer had four bullet holes in its CPU and one in the monitor. One bullet struck a filing cabinet while another made it through a wall into an adjoining room. No-one was hurt, and the unnamed man was taken for psychiatric evaluation.

FAIRFIELD

Alan Hall, 48, a pipe-fitter and Vietnam veteran, stumbled bleeding onto his front lawn in Fairfield, California, where he was spotted by a passerby who brought help. Hall was rushed to hospital, where it was discovered that his penis had been cut off; doctors were unable to reattach it. Hall, convicted in 1983 of voluntary manslaughter in the death of Denise Denofrio, told police that he had met a woman named Brenda and they had had sex in his trailer. Afterwards, Brenda hinted that the woman he had killed had been her friend, which caused him to think that she might be seeking revenge. She then cut off his penis and fled. Several women named Brenda were interviewed but after much questioning Hall admitted that he had mutilated himself with a hobby knife. He asked police not to reveal his motive.

In a similar case, 34-year-old Earl Zea from New York cut his penis off with pruning shears to discourage an unwelcome male suitor. He told police that an intruder had maimed him while he slept in his living room, but they became suspicious when no bloodstains were found.

PORTLAND

A bearded woman was shot to death in Portland, Oregon, after she was mistaken for a man. Jacqueline Anderson, 29, who had a full beard, was talking to a woman friend whose lover saw them and took her for a rival.

UTAH

Three former members of a polygamous church in Utah say that they turned £157,000 over to the sect's leader in the belief that it was the only way to meet Jesus. Angry because no such meeting had materialised, the trio is suing Jim Harmston, who heads the True and Living Church of Jesus Christ of Saints of the Last Days, for taking advantage of their "deepest spiritual needs".

DENVER

A company called My Twinn, which advertises on the internet, makes dollies like Dolly the sheep – 2ft (60cm) figures that are the spitting image of their owners. Parents send the company in Denver, Colorado, a "personal profile" and colour photographs of their child. Their technicians then mould a replica; even the clothing is copied. Prices start at about $1,600, inclusive of matching necklace and bracelet for child and doll.

My Twinn spokesman Dave Liggatt said the company got the idea from a doctor who said that when a child took a favourite toy or doll to hospital, the choice would often be based on the toy's resemblance to its owner. However, educational psychologist Jenny Smith disagreed: "I would dispute that children like dolls that look like themselves. They are not interested in such narcissistic things. This is a toy for adults, to remind them of their children when they are not there."

As if to prove her point, the company has had so many requests from women trying to relive their childhood that they have launched a "When She Was Young" range, based on photographs of the owners in their pre-teen years.

DETROIT

Police in the Detroit suburb of Warren have spent several months searching for a rare half-breed big cat, a cross between a tiger and a lion known as a liger. The animal has been reported stalking a wooded surburban area, striking fear into the hearts of local residents. Police set traps for the beast, which has been spotted on several occasions and even captured on videotape. On the tape, the animal can be see wearing a red collar, indicating that it had been kept as a pet. Michael Greiner, press secretary for the mayor of Warren, Mark Steenburgh, told residents not to approach the animal and to report any sightings to police.

One local, Sue Lacolla, told WXYZ-TV that "It's pretty scary... I was going to cut the grass today, and decided not even to do that. I'm going to keep my kids in and the dogs in the garage." Exotic cats have become a growing problem in recent years in Michigan, which does not have a law prohibiting their ownership. Detroit Zoo officials said they were housing five lion cubs abandoned or confiscated from Detroit homes in drug related cases in recent years.

BROOKLYN

A child welfare worker visited Georgina Jackson's one-room Brooklyn apartment on 22 July to investigate a report of child neglect. Jackson opened the door brandishing a table leg and tried to drag the social worker into the apartment. The unidentified social worker fled and a neighbour called the police. Jackson's children – three boys aged 15, five and 10 months and a girl of three – were living in filthy conditions with no food. The mother and the three oldest children were dressed identically in black smocks and white ceramic medallions around their necks. Police discovered that the three-year-old and five-year-old had been shaved completely and had shoulder-length blonde wigs glued to their heads. The three eldest children also wore nose rings and earrings. There was no fridge, no stove and only one mattress. All three children were malnourished, and were described as "very quiet, very polite and very withdrawn". Jackson was arrested and the children taken into care.

RHODE ISLAND

Maureen Wilcox had matching numbers in two lotteries at the same time, but won nothing. The numbers she used in the Massachusetts lottery came up in the Rhode Island draw, and her Rhode Island numbers came up in Massachusetts.

NEW JERSEY

Dr Michael Zanakis, 44, of Hardin, New Jersey, was convicted of trying to extort $5 million from MacDonald's by planting a fried rat's tail in a Happy Meal he bought for his three year-old son in Long Island. MacDonald's went to the FBI, who became suspicious when they found that Zanakis had received a $4,600 payoff from Coca-Cola in 1993 after claiming he had found "small bits of greasy particles" in a can of Coke. He had taken the tail from a medical research laboratory where he worked, had it fried and then placed it in a packet of fries. The tail came from an albino species commonly used in laboratories.

KENTUCKY

Philip Johnson of Kentucky was taken to hospital in February suffering from a gunshot wound to his left shoulder. Two years earlier, he had been treated for an identical wound, telling doctors that he "wanted to see what it felt like to get shot". The second wound was apparently also self-inflicted, because the first "felt so good he had to do it again."

FORT LAUDERDALE

Mike Babone, 34, from Fort Lauderdale, Florida, claims to have collected 95,000 signatures in an attempt to get invited onto NBC's *The Tonight Show*, an obsession born when he was 10. He has travelled more than 7,500 miles (12,070km), criss-crossing the United States and wading into crowds at football games and shopping centres with a petition which reads "Yes! I want to see Mike Babone on *The Tonight Show*! Give him his dream!" A Fort Lauderdale restaurant, Bill's Tar Pit and Ribs, is sponsoring his petition odyssey, which began some two years ago in Miami and has cost about $7,500 so far. He has vowed to continue until host Jay Leno agrees to allow him on the show. Babone is so obsessed that his wife of seven years has left him and he no longer has a job. *The Tonight Show* has no intention of booking him; a spokeswoman said that the show's producers don't want to encourage such petition drives.

DALLAS

Lauretta Adams, 43, from Dallas, Texas, had her fingernails cut recently, ending her bid to have the longest nails in the world. She had been growing them for 24 years. One was 35in (89cm) long and their combined length was 12ft 6in (381cm). She had some way to go to beat the record of 18ft 10in (574cm) held by a man in India.

THE ANIMAL WORLD

Top 10 Weird Animals

① GIANT BOA

VILLAGERS FROM Nuevo Tacna in Peru reported seeing a vast boa constrictor crashing through the jungle. The snake's size was put at 130ft (40m) long and 15ft (4.6m) across, and it reportedly left a track wide enough to drive a tractor through. The local mayor, Jorge Chavez, said that: "There were five villagers present, and the rest of the 300 villagers felt the effect of this thing as it dragged itself along and dived into the river Napo." Needless to say, the snake's dimensions would make it easily the largest ever seen.

② SPEEDY SQUIRREL

TRAFFIC SPEED cameras at Glenrothes in Fife photographed the world's fastest squirrel. The camera – which activates automatically when a speeding car passes it – snapped the squirrel halfway across an otherwise empty road. Experts said that to activate the camera, the squirrel would have needed to be running at 43mph (69kph). Tony Mitchell-Jones, a mammal ecologist with English Nature, poured cold water on the super-squirrel idea: "I'm not sure what the top speed of a squirrel is, but it's nothing like 40mph (64kph). I suspect that there is a fault with the camera." We are reliably informed that top speed for a squirrel is around 20mph (32kph) in short bursts.

www.arttoday.com

③ ICE WORMS

AMERICAN SCIENTISTS have discovered yet another previously unknown form of life, living in seemingly impossible conditions. Blind tube worms – distantly related to lugworms – have been found living in mounds of frozen methane 1,800ft (550m) under the Gulf of Mexico, an incredibly hostile environment with no light, little oxygen and high concentrations of toxins such as sulphides and concentrated brine. The inch-long (2.54cm) worms are covered in bristly "feet" and are thought to "feed" by using bacteria to extract food from the poisonous water. The worms are the latest additions to a broad group of animals known as "extremovores" which thrive in difficult conditions.

④ SQUARE-EYED CHICKS

RESEARCHERS HAVE found that television can ease the stresses of life for battery chickens. Chicks reared while watching television grow more quickly, eat less food, and lay larger eggs more regularly. Scientists at the Roslin Institute thought that television taught the chicks that novelty was not always a threat; although nervous at first, by the end of the trials they would rush to the ends of their cages to watch. They were reportedly particularly fond of the well-known "flying toasters" computer screensaver.

⑤ CATNAPPED

WHEN DEPARTMENT of Animal Regulation officers raided a suburban Los Angeles home, they discovered almost 600 cats. Most of the cats were wild or untamed, and nine were dead, with some stuffed in shopping bags and one behind a cushion on the sofa. Most were starved and weakened by infection, and 200 had to be put down soon afterwards. The owner of the house, 60-year-old Doris Romeo, had been operating a cat rescue operation called "Pets for Life", although she lived elsewhere.

⑥ FLATULENT SHEEP

NEW ZEALAND environmental scientists are conducting a survey into how flatulence in sheep affects global warming. The researchers have found a flat paddock with prevailing winds, and have built a tower downwind to measure wind strength, temperature and methane content. The sheep have been fitted with sampler devices on their noses and mouths, as 98% of the gas – which is worse in terms of global warming than the dreaded carbon dioxide – is released by belching. As well as sheep, it is produced by termites, cattle and compost heaps.

⑦ BABY SNAKES

AN AMERICAN academic has discovered at first hand that rattlesnakes can apparently reproduce without sex. David Chizar, of the University of Colorado, came into his office one morning to find that a timber rattlesnake he used in animal behaviour experiments had given birth to a litter of young male snakes. Chizar had raised the snake since it was two days old, and knew that she had never been kept with a male. After a battery of genetic tests, experts concluded that the snake had reproduced by parthenogenesis – without the need for a mate. Some other species, mostly reptiles, are able to reproduce in this way, but only give birth to males.

⑧ ALBINO PENGUIN

A YOUNG emperor penguin has been found without its "tuxedo". The first known albino penguin, it was found in the Antarctic by Gerard Kooyman of the Scripps Institute for Oceanography. Sadly, we're unlikely to hear of it again, as newly-mature penguins immediately head off on a migration of thousands of miles.

⑨ GLOBSTER

IN THE last week of 1997, a mysterious blob of decaying animal flesh – known in the fortean literature as a "globster" – was washed up on a beach in Tasmania. The four-ton lump of stinking matter was discovered by locals at Four Mile Beach in the north of the island. It was between 12 and 20 feet (3.7–6.1m) long, had a number of apparent "flippers", and was covered in coarse, spaghetti-like fibres. What was it, and where did it come from?

⑩ SLUDGE MUTANT

WORKERS AT an Indiana chemical plant discovered what appeared to be a new life-form when they cleaned out their toxic sludge pits. Several squid-like creatures were found at the Delphi Interior and Lighting Systems factory at Anderson, in vats used to store chemical waste including anti-freeze, paint stripper, oil and plastic byproducts. Witnesses said that they were around 6–8in (15–20cm) long, had tentacles and what looked like eyes, and were the same colour as an earthworm. Although a number of the creatures were found, only one was kept; it was on display in the factory, but someone stole it after a matter of weeks. State environmental regulators and the US Environmental Protection Agency confirmed that "a creature of an unknown origin or type" had been found at the plant.

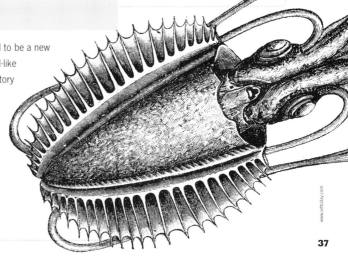

ONLY FOOLS AND GOATSUCKERS
THE SEARCH FOR THE
CHUPACABRAS

What's been sucking the life out of Latin-American livestock? With human bait in tow JON DOWNES left home looking for answers.

In early 1998, my friend Graham Inglis and I travelled to Puerto Rico in search of the truth behind El Chupacabras – the fearsome goat sucking vampire of Latin America, once described as a cross between a kangaroo and Sonic the Hedgehog on acid.

Researcher Conrad Goeringer wrote: "Believers in the Chupacabras say that the beast is a hybrid creature, in appearance something which resembles a cross between a giant dog and a lizard. It is said to walk upright on two feet, is capable of flight, and sinks its fangs into victims and kills them by drinking their blood. News reports of Chupacabras sightings come from mostly rural areas; and while the mysterious creature seems to prefer farm animals like sheep, goats, and chickens, it has been alleged to attack humans."

Attacks have been reported in Mexico, Guatemala and even the mainland United States. Our expedition took us to Puerto Rico, Mexico and Miami in the hope of tracking down some witnesses and discovering the truth about the creature.

We first spoke to a policewoman who told us how about 18 months or so before, she had been hanging out her washing on a line in the back yard – in reality an area of wasteland decorated by pampas grass and the stumps of two moth-eaten banana trees – when she had seen a spinning red light in the sky several miles away between two mountains.

Within days she had experienced a series of attacks on her poultry which were kept in a ramshackle but secure coop. On several occasions she had found members of her flock outside although they had been locked into the coop for the night. The corpses were completely drained of blood but otherwise unharmed. Some of the chickens had been covered with a revolting layer of slime which she assumed was saliva. Many researchers think that this slime is some kind of anti-coagulant – like that in the saliva of a vampire bat – which aids the exsanguination of their victims. One time she and her brother had seen the animal that they believed was responsible; bipedal and looking like a

EVIDENCE: An investigator examines the trail left by the mystery mammal in Puerto Rico.

kangaroo with spikes sticking out of its back, it had a reptilian face and slit eyes.

One of our most promising witnesses was a vet in the town of Puebla, just south of the volcano Popacatapetl. She took us to a smallholding owned by an old Mexican farmer called Dom Pedro. There were huge crucifixes daubed on the walls of Dom Pedro's farmyard and all over the walls of houses in his village. "Por protectione de vampiros".

A year before, three of his sheep had been attacked by a mysterious creature. According to a vet – the first professional on the scene – although the sheep were completely drained of blood, not breathing and their hearts not beating, they were still alive 12 hours after the attack: they reacted to light and touch stimuli, were in great pain and eventually had to be destroyed. As someone with a working knowledge of animals I found this account completely mystifying.

Whatever it is that is causing these attacks on the livestock of the region it is NOT a natural zoo predator – in Puerto Rico there are no such natural predators.

FOOTPRINTS: Evidence for the creature, or part of the tourist trade?

Rumours abound that the Chupacabras is either:

a) An introduced predator
b) An escaped exotic pet
c) A CIA-funded genetic laboratory experiment
d) Some hapless creature that has wandered into a toxic waste dump and become mutated into an unearthly monster.

There is, however, no evidence whatsoever for any of these theories.

Indeed, all the available evidence points away from them. The modus operandi of the Chupacabras killings both in Puerto Rico and elsewhere is completely different from that of any known species of predatory animal and there is no solid scientific evidence whatsoever that either spontaneous mutation or artificial chimeras could exist.

Puerto Rico is certainly a testing ground for US Government biological experiments, but these are all in the areas of pest control and involve small and unpleasant invertebrates rather than blood-sucking monsters. There are also a number of toxic waste dumps (both legal and otherwise) on the island. These have had a disastrous affect on the Puerto Rican ecosystem and have wiped out much of the endemic microfauna, but it is highly unlikely that they could have such a dramatic effect on the higher fauna of the island.

Puerto Rico is unhappy with its status as a dependent territory of the United States and, justifiably, sees itself as a testing ground for US biological experimentation and a dumping ground for its toxins. In a socio-political atmosphere such as this is there any surprise that such bizarre rumours are rampant?

There seems to be a link between the Chupacabras attacks and political/social unrest in Latin America. In Mexico both supporters of the Zapatista separatist movement and the government have used the Chupacabras as a metaphor for the activities of their political enemies.

Mexico has a long folkloric history of vampirism, and only recently have the attacks on domestic animals been blamed on El Chupacabras. Mexican ufologist Jaime Maussan told us that the early attacks were blamed on a cat-like creature. Other witnesses described an animal like a puma, sometimes with wings and usually with a strange mohican-like mane. Across Mexico City itself there are a number of gloriously baroque pieces of public statuary, and a recurrent motif is a stylised felid with a punky mane. It was only after the image of the Puerto Rican Chupacabras archetype was splashed across the world media that such an 'animal' was reported from Mexico.

The mainland USA reports that we investigated appear to have been the result of predations either by the Florida panther (an extremely rare subspecies of puma) or, perhaps even the Skunk-ape, a southern US relative of Bigfoot. Again it was only after the Puerto Rican archetype became international news that people started putting two and two together and making 666!

A final mysterious element is the footprint that I was given in Miami. The animal that reportedly made it was described as a cross between a large dog and an ape and, sure enough, when the footprint is examined closely it does appear to be akin to that of a large dog – with the fingernails of a man or an ape. Photographs of this print have been used by fortean researchers to identify the creature as a Florida panther, but having seen the artefact itself it is obvious that it is no such thing.

What is particularly interesting is that a very similar footprint was found in Rendlesham Forest in Suffolk last year – a place with a long tradition of UFO activity, animal mutilation and historical sightings of a creature known as The Shug Monkey – a bizarre hybrid of dog and ape!

Some commentators have tried to dismiss the Chupacabras as a purely Hispanic phenomenon. This is neither true nor realistic. These incidents are

ROADKILL: Could this be the Chupacabras?

merely a localised series of episodes of something that has been happening across the world for hundreds of years. El Chupacabras is far more akin to such entities as the Cornish Owlman, West Virginia's Mothman or The Jersey Devil than many mainstream ufologists and their ilk would like to believe.

If I may paraphrase both Oscar Wilde and *The X Files*, the truth may be out there but it is neither pure nor simple and in any case is open to so many avenues of interpretation that it is questionable whether any of us would recognise it if we found it.

Only Fools and Goatsuckers will be coming out through DOMRA publications, 65 Constable Road, Corby, Northants, NN18 0RT, England, later this year.

APE ATTACKS

Anyone who has ever seen *Planet of the Apes* knows who's going to be running the planet in a couple of centuries; the signs seem to be that the takeover has already started...

JAMIE HEWLETT

SEVEN ALCOHOLIC monkeys are creating havoc by raiding the Customs and Excise Department's laboratory in New Delhi. Security staff have, for several years, been unable to prevent them breaking in and stealing samples of illegal moonshine and medical alcohol brought in for testing. "Each monkey must have drunk hundreds of bottles by now," said a laboratory official. They went berserk when unable to get a drink and rampaged through the office complex, trashing everything in sight. They had even cut off the department's telephones by chewing through the lines. Plans to catch them had been futile, as the monkeys were too cunning, even when inebriated. Attempts to deal with delinquent monkeys across the country have been hampered by the reverence in which monkeys are held by Hindus, who associate them with the monkey god Hanuman.

A SIMILAR situation lead to a novel solution in the northern Indian state of Punjab. Here a jail for monkeys has been opened in response to the rising number of attacks on humans. Wild monkeys are captured on the streets and kept locked up until they are declared fit for release. Some victims have even been 'mugged' for their handbags. Two blocks of the Indian government buildings have become home to gangs of monkeys which attack unwary officials, and the All India

Institute of Medical Sciences has to keep its windows locked for fear of invasion by the descendants of escaped lab monkeys. Attempts to cull the monkeys have been hampered by an export ban and by respect for Hanuman.

A PACK of macaque monkeys terrorised the seaside resort of Ito, on the Izu peninsula, about 60 miles (97km) south-west of Tokyo, in late January, attacking 30 people and sending eight of them to hospital with bites. The victims, 26 of whom were women between the ages of 40 and 80, were attacked from behind, often in their own homes, by monkeys who bit them on the ankles, calves and backs. One woman, 62, was bitten in her living room; another was jumped on the street and pushed to the ground. Officials in the town have no idea why the usually peaceful monkeys came down from the mountains, but suggest that an unusually snowy winter has forced them into town to scavenge. However, this doesn't explain their aggression or why they mostly targeted women. At least five monkeys, each standing as high as 3.3ft (1m), were spotted tangled in laundry, breaking into homes and going for the ceremonial fruit on Buddhist altars. The town fought back. At one school, a "monkey patrol" guarded

the building with long sticks to swat away any monkeys which came near the children. Loudspeaker messages, which normally announce impending earthquakes, warned people to keep their doors locked and not to feed the monkeys. Local hunters were being recruited to scare the animals back into the mountains with air rifles.

A TROUPE of about 60 gorillas invaded the village of Olamze on the border with Equatorial Guinea looking for an infant gorilla which had been seized earlier in the day by local hunter Ntsama Ondo. Shortly before midnight, the gorillas entered the village in single file, ignoring gun-shots fired by villagers to scare them away, before retiring into the jungle. The next night they came back, and this time they beat on the doors and windows of dwellings. Faced with the determination of the gorillas to recover the captive youngster and learning who was responsible, the village chief ordered Ntsama Ondo to release his prisoner. According to the Cameroon newspaper *L'Action*: "the assailants returned to the forest with shouts of joy, savouring their victory".

TRULY MAN'S **BEST** FRIEND

Normally, it's humans who have to come to the rescue of animals – firemen helping kittens stuck in trees and the like. Sometimes however, the tables are turned...

MISTY HARGER, 12, was out walking with her 11-year-old sister and foster parents when she wandered off into the woods bordering the canyon of the Buffalo river in the Arkansas wilderness. Two hours later she was found by Scotty, the family's scruffy mongrel. The dog followed the disorientated girl as she went deeper and deeper into the forest, and stayed with her as a police helicopter with heat-seeking equipment and 100 searchers with bloodhounds tried in vain to find her. When Misty took off her shoes because they had got wet, Scotty took them away and hid them, preventing her from walking further and, perhaps, falling into the fast-flowing river. Dressed in light clothing, Misty would almost certainly have died had she fallen asleep during the night, when temperatures dipped to minus 8°C (17.6°F). But she was not only kept warm by Scotty, but also awake by his almost constant barking at a mysterious white owl perched nearby that "kind of glowed". Finally, 24 hours after getting lost and 90 minutes before a snowstorm blanketed the area, Misty was found by rescuers searching the river by boat. She was flown to hospital, but released when she was found to be in good health. Meanwhile, Scotty slipped away amid the excitement and trotted home. Undoubtedly, the mongrel had saved Misty's life. Ken Hilton, her foster father, said he did not believe it was coincidence that Scotty found Misty. "We know God had a hand in protecting her," he said. Sgt Bolen of the Searcy county sheriff's department said: "I don't know of any white owls in the county. That's some kind of sign."

A NEW-BORN baby abandoned in sub-zero temperatures by his mother in Bucharest, the Romanian capital, was saved by a pack of wild dogs. Two of the dogs stood guard over the tiny bundle while two others attracted police officers with their barking. The boy was found covered in fallen leaves, with the remains of his umbilical cord and placenta still attached. It was thought that a dog had licked the baby's body clean. The child was adopted by one of the policemen.

IT HAPPENED again in Romania soon after, in the village of Salistea. A naked premature baby, weighing 3.7lbs (1,678g), was dumped by its mother in freezing weather in a neighbour's garden. Pet pooch Dana dragged the baby into a barn where she was suckling her pups and kept it warm until Dana's owner found the child. At the time of the report, the child, recovering in an incubator, was to be reunited with its mother, a 32-year-old woman apparently carrying the names of goddesses – Diana Minerva. The mother of six was being treated for depression after telling police she had dumped the baby because she had no money.

BJORN VIDAR Marthinussen, 29, and his stepsons were asleep when their house in the Norwegian town of Rognan caught fire. Argo, the family's four-year-old German shepherd, who had never shown a mastery of door handles before, managed to open two doors and race upstairs to wake the family. All escaped just before flames engulfed the house.

AT FOUR o'clock one morning, Roc, a mix of retriever and Rottweiler, spotted a fire sparked by lightning in the attic of his owners' house in New Bern, North Carolina. His barking failed to wake them, so he rang the doorbell. Roosevelt and Linda Matthews and their two teenage children lost everything but their lives in the fire. Roc won their eternal gratitude. The dog was never trained by the family to ring doorbells, though he had done it once before to get their attention.

DONNA, A four-year-old retriever, saved the life of her master Sture Abrahamsson in January, when his house in the Swedish village of Halland burnt down. He was asleep on the sofa in front of the TV when Donna barked and pulled his ear. Just in time, he smashed a window and jumped out – with the dog – before the house was completely destroyed. The fire was probably caused by a short-circuiting fan heater. Donna usually slept in the horses' stable some 50 yards from the house, but on that particular night she had dodged into the house.

ED TRAQUINO

MUTANTS and hybrids

DOBSON AGENCY

Pollution in the environment? Dangerous solar radiation? Or just some frisky animals without something of the right species in the area?
You decide...

LEOPARD THAT LOST ITS SPOTS

OXFORDSHIRE'S COTSWOLD Safari Park is now home to an extremely rare black leopard. The cub, called Indigo, has a brother, born at the same time as her and named Ramu, who has the normal leopard spots. Indigo is thought to be the only black Siberian leopard in the world. Her parents were normally spotted Amurs from Frankfurt Zoo. Peter Jackson, chairman of the Cat Specialist Group, which oversees the breeding of big cats in captivity, said: "We suspect that Indigo's father was not pure Siberian. He might be part Nepalese leopard, and that could account for the black cub. There may be as few as 22 of these leopards left in Russia, 15 in China and a few in North Korea. They are in a desperate situation."

PIG-HEADED

RUDY, AN eight-month old pig with two snouts but only two ears, has been bought for $5,000 from Scott Vorwald of Marquette, Iowa, by Pigs Without Partners – a Los Angeles-based animal rescue group – in order to save him from a life in a circus sideshow. The porcine prodigy weighs 150lb (68kg); what looks like a Cyclops-like middle eye turned out to be just a cavity with a fold of skin. The peculiar piggy is to be adopted by a woman with a 750-acre ranch east of Santa Barbara, California, where he will join four other pigs, including a dwarf and a pig with a bad bladder. Experts say it is rare for a pig with such deformities to survive birth.

IT'LL BE ALL WHITE ON THE NIGHT

Bill Coppersmith had seen some weird lobsters in his 20 years of fishing, but even he was surprised when he hauled in an albino lobster off Casco Bay, Maine, on 10 November. "When the trap broke the water, it just glowed... It was almost like a toy," he said of the 9in (23cm) long, 1lb (500g) crustacean, which he estimated to be about 20 years old and nicknamed Lincoln (or Lionel – reports differ). White lobsters are extremely rare, not least because they are conspicuous and easy prey for predators. Robert Bayer, Director of the University of Maine's Lobster Institute, said he had seen one other albino lobster about 15 years

POPPERFOTO

ago, near Kittery on the New Hampshire border. Lobsters usually have dark green shells, but occasionally are blue or yellow. The shell turns red when cooked. Mr Bayer speculated that, if boiled, Lincoln would turn a light grey. Mr Coppersmith kept the white prodigy in a tank at his seafood store in Raymond, Maine, while he fielded questions from mass media across the USA and around the world. Lincoln was eventually auctioned to an aquarium for £15,000.

As if to mock the pronouncement that albino lobsters were extraordinarily rare, two more turned up around the same time. One nicknamed Barry was caught off Filey in North Yorkshire in early November and now lives at the Sea Life Centre in Scarborough, where it was insured for £20,000.

At the beginning of December, a third turned up at Bernard Warner's fishmonger shop in Doncaster, South Yorkshire, as part of a routine delivery. It was two and a half times the normal size and covered in barnacles.

Deciding it was simply suffering from old age, Mr Warner flew off to Madeira on holiday. There he learned from the press about the other two lobsters and their extraordinary value. He raced to a phone after touching down. "Don't sell that lobster", he told Brenda, his sister-in-law. It was too late: it had gone for £16.50, boiled and digested by an unknown diner. Mr Warner, who had worked in the family business for 40 years, had never come upon an albino lobster before. "Someone has had a very valuable meal without even knowing it", he said. "For me it's like winning the lottery and then discovering you have thrown the ticket away."

IT'S GWAN IN A MILLION

THIS HYBRID or "gwan", thought to be the offspring of a black swan and a domestic goose, was found in Sunninghill, near Ascot in Berkshire. Although it has the graceful neck of a swan, the bill, tetchy waddle, and smooth feathers are all charcteristic of a goose – and it honks. "It would be exceptional for a goose and a swan to interbreed, but there is no doubt that it has happened here," said Jon Bowler, a research officer at the Slimbridge Wildfowl and Wetlands Trust in Gloucestershire. Cross-breeding can occur when one of the parents becomes "imprinted" by birds of the other parent's species. The most likely explanation is that a swan's egg had hatched in a group of young geese, or vice versa, and the gwan's parent grew up feeling it was a member of the other species. The gwan (or swoose), dubbed 'Poppet' and believed to be about 10 years old, was put in a pen with mute swans and was not aggressive. It is likely to be a one-off as hybrids are usually infertile.

HOPPING MAD

THE NORTH Arnerican Reporting Genter for Amiphibian Malformations has received reports of frog mutants from three Canadian provinces and 38 US states since mid-1995. Understanding the cause of the increase in reports of frogs with missing, deformed or misplaced limbs was brought a little nearer by confirmation from the US Environmental Protection Agency's Mid-Continent Ecology Division in Duluth, Minnesota, that the developmental abnormalities were more llkely to have been caused by increased exposure to ultraviolet radiation than to pesticides. Steven Heake, acting director of the EPA facility, stressed that their findings are preliminary and have not confirmed that seasonal ozone layer depletion may be the cause. Not everyone agrees. At a San Francisco meeting of the Society of Environmental Toxicology and Chemistry in November, pesticides, leaking landfills, parasites and even tadpole cannibalism were named as possible culprits.

DOGGIE STYLE

A ONE-year-old stray puppy found in Middlesbrough, Cleveland, and named Jasper, is part corgi (short and fluffy) and part rottweiler (big and ferocious). "He is without doubt the product of a rottweiler bitch and a corgi dog because the other way round lust wouldn't be possible," said Kate Wilson, the kennel owner who rescued the curious canine. He is l8in (46cm) tall and 24in (61 cm) long and has the rottweiler's sharp teeth, ears and tail. His bark is much deeper than a corgi's.

ED TRAQUINO

ANIMALS
BEHAVING BADLY

It's not just humans who behave badly after a few drinks. This crop of animals under the influence demonstrates that creatures of all sizes, from elephants to birds, like a tipple – and not all of them can hold their drink.

A YOUNG cow elk, thoroughly intoxicated on fermented apples, caused a lot of trouble in the village of Munka-Ljungby, near Helsingborg in Sweden. After she had chased the guests attending Ann-Mari Fröderberg's birthday party, five police cars arrived in time to see the roaring animal chase a mother and child into a house. The elk became very upset when the nine policemen attempted to get her out of the village. Eventually she got tired of the excitement and staggered off into the forest to sleep it off. The Swedish papers are full of similar tales of elks behaving badly every year around November.

ELEPHANTS IN the Himalayan foothills and elsewhere constantly raid liquor supplies. Around Christmas 1997, a herd of about 25 elephants came trumpeting down from the hills to the Bangladeshi village of Dighakon, near Jamalpur, and broke into the distillery of the local Gara tribe. In their drunken rampage, they flattened the entire village, forcing frightened villagers to flee as buildings came crashing down.

IN RECENT years, elephants have regularly made off with scores of bottles of rum from a supply base in the jungle area of Bagdogra, north Bengal. They douse fires lit to scare them away and short-circuit electric fences with uprooted trees. Once inside the depot, the huge raiders make short work of the thin steel railings and wooden windows to get at the rum, sugar, flour and bananas inside. They break the bottles by curling their trunks around them and smashing off the necks. The pesky pachyderms then sway around enjoying themselves before returning to the jungle. It is not advisable to offer any resistance. One elephant never forgot the man who poured hot water on him one night – and returned regularly to demolish his hut.

IN MOSCOW, marauding rats have for years been breaking into storerooms, where they open vodka bottles with their teeth. Rat packs in New Delhi spent December drinking gallons of illicit alcohol seized by police, then biting people and even attacking cats kept to control them. This was particularly embarrassing for the police, because the rats were drinking evidence due to be produced in court.

AFTER CONSUMING fermented berries in Iowa City last November, a flock of cedar wax wings were killed when they flew into shop windows. Later, about 30 were observed still clinging unsteadily to the berry tree, while 40 were lying unconscious beneath it.

JEREMY JESSEL, out walking his dog on Tooting Bec Common in London early one morning, was alerted by a disturbance behind a bush. He found three crows sloshing into a can of strong beer. All were bleary-eyed, argumentative and staggering about on their claws. One grabbed the can and tried unsuccessfully to fly off with it. Mr. Jessel, of The Balham Society, regarded the episode as shocking evidence of the decline in contemporary manners. "In the good old days," he mused, "one never used to see a stoned crow until after lunch."

IN SRI LANKA farmers are frequently kept awake by the raucous all-night raves of drunken rats, bats and monkeys who have over-indulged in toddy, the local drink made from coconut nectar and hung up in jars on coconut palms to ferment. The animals do a lot of damage upsetting the jars. S. A. Senadhi, of the Sri Lankan Society for Environmental Education, conducting a butterfly survey, noticed clusters of the creatures hanging round a plant known as the "elephant's trunk". Dew had fermented on the plant's berries, producing an intoxicating brew. The butterflies stayed on the plant for several days. By the end, many had damaged wings, most were "sloppy and lazy" and some were so blotto that they couldn't be bothered to move when disturbed.

ED TRAQUINO

TASMAN GLOBSTER

The venerable fortean enigma of "globsters" – huge, mysterious lumps of decaying tissue washed up on beaches – raised its wobbly head again in early January. An enormous, stinking blob of fibrous matter was discovered on Tasmania's Four Mile Beach on around the 5th; weighing in at around four tonnes and 20ft (6.1m) long (initial reports suggested 12ft (3.7m)), the creature sported what appeared to be a large number of paddle-like flippers. It was covered in coarse, spaghetti-like fibres, generally referred to in reports as "hair". Physically, it bore a strong resemblance to a smaller animal washed up in Benbecula in 1992. This one was roughly tadpole-shaped, with the "head" end around 3ft (1m) high; the body appeared to be around 4ft (1.2m) across, with several "flippers" along one side, each about 1ft (30cm) long.

This latest casualty turned up some time in the first week of January, and was dragged above the high tide mark by locals. Nobody in the area was able to identify it – as one local memorably put it: "I've seen

deformed sharks and other fish, but never anything like this... It's just repulsive" – so speculation as to its origin ran high. While those who had actually seen the mystery mass up close wouldn't say much beyond "we just can't identify it," the press let rip: the *Sun* and the *Daily Record* compared it to "a cross between a squid and a walrus"; the *Daily Mail* suggested a dinosaur or the roots of a mangrove tree; *The Scotsman* soberly suggested it might be a basking shark.

A ranger from the Arthur River Parks and Wildlife Service, Jamie Baylystark, told reporters: "it is most likely that a whale died somewhere at sea, and pieces of the blubber washed up on the beach. As whale blubber dries, it begins to appear quite fibrous, and once it becomes covered in sand, can appear hairy." His suspicions were confirmed within the week, when Barry Bruce, a marine biologist from CSIRO Marine Research in Hobart, examined the globster. He was happy to identify the remains as whale blubber, but was willing to take the investigation further with a DNA analysis: "It's important that we

establish the species of whale and therefore provide a more accurate record on strandings to remove some of the mystery in future."

Globsters have been reported for years. Charles Fort mentioned one suspect but noteworthy account from Margate, South Africa wh,ich claimed that the globster had been observed in a titanic struggle with two whales. According to an eyewitness account, it was killed by the whales and its body washed ashore, where it remained for ten days. In this case, the body was dragged to below the high tide mark once the smell of decay became unbearable, and washed away in the night.

Other mystery blobs have been found previously around Australasia. One well-known example washed ashore at Temma, also in Tasmania, in 1960 and was similarly identified as whale blubber – although locals disputed this, claiming that the investigative team had simply stumbled upon another enormous lump of reeking flesh in the same area which had gone previously unnoticed.

EASY AS ABC
CATS
IN A FLAP

While the government continues to pussyfoot around reports of mysterious felines, we present the *Fortean Times'* round-up of Alien Big Cat sightings.

PHIL BOND

The big news of the year – in the Alien Big Cat world at least – was the appearance of video footage claiming to show the ever-elusive "Beast of Bodmin". The 20-second video shows two separate black animals walking through unidentified moorland, said to be near Jamaica Inn, south-west of Launceston. The first appears to be about 3ft (90cm) in length, while the second, seen face-on, is said to resemble a large, muscular domestic cat. Mike Thomas, managing director of Newquay Zoo, maintains that the second animal's golden eyes and rounded tail suggest that it isn't a domestic cat. The film was shot by a local man, identified only as "John", who had seen a large black cat slip through a hedge on the moor's edge, and had returned regularly to the spot in the hope of further sightings.

Our main survey was compiled from 304 press cuttings sent in by *Fortean Times* readers. The nation's most ubiquitous crypto-mammal manifested in 31 counties in England, as well as in Ireland, Scotland and Wales.

As usual, the majority of witnesses described a large black (or dark brown) cat, about the size of a Labrador, 18-30in (45-80cm) tall, with a body 2-4ft (60-120cm) in length, and a long tail.

Since the inconclusive 1995 report on the "Beast of Bodmin" by MAFF (the Ministry of Agriculture, Fisheries and Food), national press coverage of Cornish ABCs has been low-key, but things perked up last summer. On 29 August, three quarrymen spotted two ABCs, at least 6ft (1.8m) long, one black, one grey, from 20 yards (18m), walking across the bottom of the disused Blue Barrow China Clay Pit in Roche, about 7 miles (11km) SW of Bodmin.

Five weeks later, there was a sighting about three miles (4.8km) to the south. A party of 20 county councillors was on an annual coach trip to various sites in the county recently given planning permission. At 11am on 3 October, as they passed the disused clay pits at Starric Moor near Stenalees, Cllr Sue Swift saw a large dark brown cat drinking from a pool.

She pointed this out to Planning Committee Chairman Joan Vincent and three other councillors. Mrs Vincent returned with her husband and found paw prints, some 5in (13cm) wide and some smaller. Mike Thomas declared the prints were "conclusive proof" of a puma with a cub or cubs, after comparing them with prints made by his captive pumas.

On 27 November, the Cornish Guardian published a photo of two ABCs, one tawny, one darker brown, taken through binoculars near the coast in the St Austell area the previous January. The photographer was known to *Cornish Guardian* editor Alan Cooper, but wished to keep his name and the location of the photograph secret, so that the animals were not disturbed. He did not seek payment. "My wife and I saw the creatures on Christmas Day last year [1996]," he said. "We saw them again two weeks later and several times afterwards until they disappeared with the arrival of holidaymakers around Easter. At all times they appeared around an hour or two after daybreak on cold sunny mornings. They seem to use the area for a bit of sunbathing."

He also photographed paw prints on the coastal sand nearby, alongside those of a large dog for comparison. Newquay Zoo's Mike Thomas

WESTERN MAIL

A sheep carcass on a Welsh fence? Is this an example of big cat depredation?

identified the tawny animal in the photograph as an adult female puma, possibly pregnant – the branch across the standing animal's back was 2ft (60cm) off the ground, according to the photographer. Others said the photo showed two domestic cats, while Di Francis, author of *Cat Country* declared the picture to show an indigenous British big cat.

A curious prelude to the episode was played out a month earlier. On 25 October the *News of the World* was preparing to run a front page scoop of Bodmin Beast photographs when deputy editor Rebekah Wade became suspicious and confronted the reporter and photographer responsible. The photographer, who was fired from the paper, now claims he was ordered to fake the photographs, but his ex-employers deny that such a "culture of fabrication" exists.

Five ewes were found savaged near the councillors' Starric Moor ABC sighting in mid-November and North Cornwall MP Paul Tyler called for a re-opening of the MAFF enquiry. On Boxing Day, Countryside Minister Eliot Morley agreed to a fresh investigation.

Two other MPs were demanding that the government investigate the ABC situation in their constituencies: Keith Simpson (Mid Norfolk) and Cynog Dafis (Ceredigion and Pembroke North). The extent of sheep depredation by the "Beast of Bont" around Aberystwyth in Wales is familiar from previous surveys. On one night last November, 40 sheep at Mynydd Epynt, between Brecon and Sennybridge, were killed with a clean bite to the neck.

The number of sightings and livestock kills around Norwich took a distinct upturn. For instance, on 25 March 1997, a ewe was found mutilated and partially eaten in

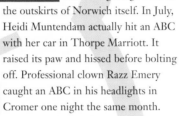

Mike Thomas matched this Cornish paw print with his captive puma's.

PAUL ARMIGER

Bawburgh near Norwich. Claw marks on its back and a gaping hole in its neck were thought to be sure signs of an ABC. The mauled body of a lamb was found at Beetley, near Dereham, on 25 October. The skull was thoroughly chewed and the back completely skinned. In December the Norwich police said that the "Norfolk Gnasher" had been seen at least 54 times since the beginning of July. Several sightings were in the outskirts of Norwich itself. In July, Heidi Muntendam actually hit an ABC with her car in Thorpe Marriott. It raised its paw and hissed before bolting off. Professional clown Razz Emery caught an ABC in his headlights in Cromer one night the same month.

A large brownish cat was seen crapping near Great Torrington in Devon on 17 November and droppings were collected for DNA analysis. It had been hoped that the test results would be announced in January 1998, but the team of scientists at Leicester University under Professor Sir Alec Jeffreys said their findings were inconclusive and they needed more time.

On six occasions in 1997, ABCs were seen by three people at once. At 8.30am on 2 January, three Kettering refuse collectors – Milan Krajcir, Ivan Thornley and Sharod Piggin – saw a 6.5ft (2m) black ABC in the snow at 100ft (30m) at Great Cransley, Northamptonshire. They followed it across a field before losing sight of it near a wood.

On 4 August, the witnesses were three members of the Peace family at Appleby Magna in Leicestershire. In September, Peter Bexfield, his mother-in-law Hilda Hall and her neighbour Albert Morris saw an enormous lion-like white cat at Lyneal Mill Cottages, near Ellesmere in Shropshire.

On 25 September, Fife Council workers David Maguire, Jack Marr and Bill Cowan were strimming grass on Kilrenny Common near Anstruther when they saw a black ABC on three occasions between 10.45am and noon. Mr Marr was a particularly good witness, being a natural historian and author of many articles on wildlife.

The closest sighting by a trio of witnesses occurred in Llanrhystud, near Aberystwyrth, West Wales. Rhodri Shaw, Rhys Davies and Sion Evans, all 12, were camping near their homes on 29 August when they heard a noise and saw a silhouette of an animal on their tent. "We thought it was a small cat magnified by moonlight," said Rhodri. "But when we looked out, we saw this huge black cat 2.5ft [76cm] tall. We froze as it circled the tent." The oddest ABC sighting was on 24 November on Blue Bell Hill in Kent (scene of the famous phantom jaywalker). The witness was driving towards Chatham when he saw what he took to be a big ostrich on grassland to the left of the A229. Then he thought it was some kind of bird scarer. Finally, he realised it was a dark cat-like creature and he pulled over onto the hard shoulder for a closer look. It quickly disappeared into undergrowth. After the report in *Kent Today*, a witness rang in to say he had seen what looked like a gorilla in the same area several years ago and a family reported a sighting of a black ABC. Besides the various human phantoms, there seems to be a veritable fortean menagerie on Blue Bell Hill.

Is this the Beast of Blue Bell Hill? Snapped in fields at Cooling, near Rochester, Kent

HARRY MATTHEWS/KENT MESSENGER

WHY ARMADILLOS DIE HARDER

WHEN THE nine-banded armadillo is frightened, it launches itself vertically into the air, a defence reaction that may frighten off predators, but leads to heavy road casualties – instead of cars passing right over it, it is hit full on by the grille. The roadsides of northern Florida are littered with armadillo carcasses, a resource put to unexpected use by Dr Diane Kelly of Duke University in Durham, North Carolina. Dr Kelly has discovered that the penis of the nine-banded armadillo has a structure never previously identified in any organ. The chances are, she believes, that all mammalian penises, including those of humans, are similarly constructed, but that nobody has noticed.

Erections are achieved by internal fluid pressure acting against a rigid sheath, composed of fibres that run up and down the organ. Dr Kelly's discovery, published in the *Journal of Morphology*, is that, in the armadillo at least, these reinforcing fibres are arranged not as spirals running helically around the organ, but in two sets at right angles to one another, like scaffolding. Such an orthogonal array of fibres provides maximal resistance to buckling, clearly an advantage in a penis. Fracture is not impossible but thankfully rare. Dr Kelly proved this by inflating armadillo penises and testing them to buckle-point.

FEATHERED FIEND

POLICE FROM Melksham, Wiltshire, rushed to answer an emergency call only to find that it had been made by a bird. Sammy the parakeet had dialled the number by jumping repeatedly on the number nine button on a phone while his owner, a Mrs Fisher, was out of the room. The puzzled Mrs Fisher let the police in, and brought them into the sitting room. As they talked, she noticed that her phone was slightly off the hook and realised what must have happened.

ANIMALS
DYING, FLYING & LYING

FABRICE

AN ESSEX couple found themselves confronted with a surreal scene when a tortoise they had thought was dead proved lively enough to dig itself out of its grave. Martin and Eileen Cattell, from Hullbridge, Essex, had acquired Tommy from a relative's garden 23 years ago. Tommy disappeared on 10 August and was found, about 20 hours later, at the bottom of their 2ft 6in (190cm)-deep garden pond. He was thought to have fallen from a lily pad. His head and legs were hanging limply out of his shell while his eyes were open and staring. The Cattells left him on the lawn for half an hour, but he did not stir; so they dug a 2ft (60cm) grave near a bay tree and laid him to rest.

However, he began to stir in the evening while Mrs Cattell was watering the garden. "It was like a scene from a horror film," she said. "Out of the corner of my eye I saw the earth move and a leg appear. I screamed and my husband pulled him out." Tommy did not appear to have learned from his 30-hour burial – he had to be rescued from the pond again within hours of his resurrection.

AN UNNAMED pensioner called the Meteorological Office at Bracknell on 4 March to inform them that an early-morning shower over her house in Shirley, Croydon, south London, had been accompanied by a large number of dead frogs. The unlucky frogs were scattered over her garden, her neighbour's house, and nearby streets. As no-one at the Met Office had the presence of mind to note down her name, the woman has proved impossible to trace. Another local said his dog was trying to eat the creatures as he took it for a walk.

Met Office spokesman Andy Yeatman was willing to offer, in best fortean fashion, a number of possible explanations for the latest report. "We know there was a heavy rain that night," he told us, "so it could have triggered a migration of frogs – it wouldn't be unprecedented, as it's been observed before." However, the woman does seem to have seen the frogs actually falling along with the rain and, moreover, they were all dead, which seems to count that theory out. Yeatman also offered the traditional waterspout explanation – that the frogs were picked up somewhere by a mini-tornado and dropped some miles away. However, as has often been the objection in the past, it is a rare tornado that can pick up one type of animal from a pool to the exclusion of all others.

 IN A unique moment in animal research, Yorkshire Television enabled Dr Richard Wiseman of the University of Hertfordshire to carry out a million-viewer lie detection test. Presenter Carolyn Hodge told viewers she never had a pet as a child because she has asthma. Then she said she loved pets and once had a guinea pig called Crumpet. Viewers were invited to guess which was the truth by ringing yes/no phone numbers, with one pair of numbers for left-handed people and one for right. Out of almost 5,000 calls, 1,564 were left-handed and 3,342 right-handed. While 72.5 per cent of right-handers guessed correctly that there had been a guinea pig in Carolyn Hodge's life, only 66 per cent of southpaws got it right. Right-handers tend to use the brain's left hemisphere, which is where linguistic information is processed. "Lots of the clues in the clips were to do with language," said Dr Wiseman. "When the presenter was lying, there was little detail. When she was telling the truth there was lots of detail." He also thought that right-handers were better at interpreting the emotional signals coming from liars.

WINGS OF CHANCE

A FLIGHT by a bird of prey ended in a quite staggering coincidence... or perhaps an example of avian precognition. Yaska (below), a three-month-old female Lanner falcon, escaped from her tether near Tunbridge Wells at the beginning of July. She was bred by leading conservationist Eddie Hare and escaped when he tripped while handling her at his bird of prey sanctuary, a stately home called Groombridge Place. Two-and-a-half weeks later, on 21 July, Yaska turned up 300 miles (483km) away at Great Harwood, near Clitheroe in Lancashire. She was rescued by falconer Peter Wall after being found in a hedge a quarter of a mile (400m) from his home. A few days earlier, Mr Wall had telephoned Mr Hare, whom he had never met, to arrange a visit to Groombridge Place. The meeting was fixed for 22 July and, the night before, Mr Wall was about to telephone Mr Hare to confirm his visit when he was called out to Yaska by a local gamekeeper. When he got home with the bird, he telephoned the number engraved on the leg ring and found he was speaking to the man whom he was about to phone. "I saved myself a phone call and he saved himself a trip to Clitheroe to pick Yaska up," said Mr Wall. He took Yaska back to Tunbridge Wells the next day.

TOM SMITH

VIRTUALLY DEAD

AN ULTRA-ORTHODOX rabbi in the northern Israeli town of Safed has ruled that tamagotchi virtual pets must fend for themselves on the Sabbath. He gave the decision to a strictly observant Jewish youth who was annoyed that he had to let his tamagotchi "die" every week.

DEVIL DUCK

A DUCK collided with a minibus in Kinshasa, the Congoles capital, shattering its windscreen and showering the passengers with glass, according to the daily *La Tempête des Tropiques*. When the duck landed unharmed on a passenger's lap, angry commuters surrounded the bird and cursed it as a devil. The driver rescued the duck, but took it to the nearest police station "to see justice done".

INSECT REPELLENT

THE LATEST pet craze in Queensland, Australia, is giant cockroaches over 3in (7.6cm) long. *Macropanesthia rhinoceros* are 30 times heavier than the typical house cockroach, are wingless and eat only dead leaves. Kids can pick them up and cuddle them before putting them back in a box.

FRUITY FROG

WHEN KEVIN Bastarache peeled an orange he had bought at his local store in Cornierville, New Brunswick, Canada, out hopped an orange-coloured frog just over an inch (3cm) long. Two days later, an expert identified it as a Pacific tree frog, found along the American west coast from California to British Colombia. It remained a mystery how the frog (which has since died) got inside the orange. Bonnie Gallant of the Magnetic Hill Zoo said that Bastarache must have overlooked an entry hole (in an orange as he peeled it?). Valmond Melanson, owner of the store where Bastarache bought the orange, said he had never heard of such a story before and promised to call his supplier in Quebec.

STRANGE EUROPE

ENGLAND v HOLLAND

Fervent Eurosceptics took a body blow when leading cricket experts agreed that this most English of games may have originated in Holland and been imported to Britain by the French. The claim was advanced by John Eddowes in his book *The Language of Cricket*, which was regarded favourably by both Christopher Martin-Jenkins, cricket editor of the *Daily Telegraph*, and Matthew Engel, editor of "the cricketers' bible" *Wisden Cricketers' Almanack*.

The earliest mentions of the game in England mirror the settlement here of cloth-workers from Flanders and northern France during the 14th century. One cluster of set-tlements centred on Guildford, where the first written mention of cricket is officially recorded. In 1589, John Derrick gave evidence during a court case about a parcel of land that, as a young man, "he and diverse of his fellowes did runne and play there at creckett and other plaies."

Eddowes quotes from *The Flemish Ancestry of Early English Ball Games: The Cumulative Evidence* by Dr Heiner Gillmeister: "The early term of cricket goes back to a Flemish phrase *met de krik ketsen*, literally 'to chase with a stick'. This was shortened to krikets, which finally became cricket." In the Bodleian Library in Oxford, Mr Eddowes found a detail from a 14th-century Flemish manuscript depicting a nun throwing a ball at a monk, who is preparing to hit it with a stick in front of what appears to be a cordon of monastic slip fielders. Furthermore, "stump" is in Dutch "stomp" but is not found any-where in Anglo-Saxon.

POBRA DO CARAMIÑAL

Juan Villasante, a street-sweeper in the village of Pobra do Caramiñal in northwestern Spain, was persuaded to part with 70p for a lottery ticket while out drinking with a friend; only two tickets remained unsold at the time. A few hours later, Villasante, who was 76, dropped dead of a heart attack on his way to see a doctor to arrage a cataract operation.

That night, four lucky customers of the Bar Chispa found they had each won £20,000; the fifth winning ticket had gone to Villasante. His niece, Maria Antonia Alonso. only learned about the win after her uncle's funeral. She and her family searched his home in vain; there wasn't even any mention of ticket 79893 among the possessions returned to them from the clinic where he died.

As he was buried in the suit he was wearing when he bought the ticket, it was widely believed that he had been buried with it in his pocket. Maria Antonia asked the local magistrate to interrogate anyone who was with the man when he died, and even to exhume the body if necessary. Meanwhile, a police guard was put on his grave to deter would-be graverobbers.

About 10 days later, it was revealed that the ticket had been cashed, but no-one knew by whom.

COPENHAGEN

Copenhagen's famous Little Mermaid statue was beheaded at the start of the year. The small bronze statue, depicting the character from Hans Christian Andersen's fairy tale, has perched on a rock in Copenhagen harbour since 1913, and has often attracted paint and grafitti attacks in the past. It has even been beheaded before, in 1964. On that occasion, the responsibility was claimed by a number of different people and groupings, including the Danish artist Jorgen Nash, who had been thrown out of the Situationist International two years earlier. The head was never found, and a new one had to be cast. The mermaid also lost an arm in 1986.

This time, an anonymous phone tip-off came to freelance cameraman Michael Poulsen, who arrived in time to videotape two young men rollerskating into the distance and taunting him with cries of "You're too late!" The following day, a previously unknown group calling themselves the Radical Feminist Faction claimed responsibility, saying the statue was "a symbol of hostility to women and of men's sexually-obsessed dreams in which women are only bodies with no head." They retracted their claim the following day.

After less than a week, a box containing the head was dumped by a hooded man outside a television station in Skovlunde, 12 miles (19k) west of the capital. The drop-off was filmed by Poulsen, following another anonymous tip-off. The restored statue was unveiled in February, while Poulsen has been arrested by police and charged with complicity in vandalism.

MOSCOW

Moscow is buzzing with excitement over rumours that the legendary "lost library" of Ivan the Great has been found. 87-year-old Moscow pensioner Apalos Ivanov claims that he has tracked the archive down, and has visited a maze of tunnels beneath the Kremlin in which he discovered the long-lost resting place of a unique treasury of manuscripts and books.

The library was lost during the reign of Ivan IV – the Terrible – who died in 1584. It was assembled by his grandfather, Ivan the Great, and consists mainly of Hebrew, Latin and Egyptian manuscripts which came to Russia in the company of Sphia Palæologa, Ivan the Great's wife and niece of the last Byzantine emperor, Constantine XI. It is also thought to contain some of the earliest books written in Russian.

There is ample evidence that the library actually did exist, since Ivan IV ordered the translation of several of its volumes into Russian. Howver, its history is somewhat murky; according to legend, it filled three huge halls, and was so valued that Ivan IV had it hidden in a vault to protect it from the fires which plagued Moscow. Nobody seems entirely sure what happened to it after his death. Some scholars believe that it was destroyed by fire shortly afterwards, while others think it may have been removed and taken to Sergeyev Posad, 50 miles (80km) away, where Ivan reigned prior to his death.

Wherever the library ended up, it has been sought for the past 400 years by scores of scholars, without success. A major obstacle was, inevitably, the security of the Kremlin; searches were banned for many years after the assassination of Sergei Kirov in 1934. Ivanov is popularly believed to have discovered the truth since he is blind – tradition has it that this fate will befall anyone who learns of the library's whereabouts.

LILLE

3,000 people were evacuated from the Eurocity tower in the French city of Lillle after it was shaken by bizarre vibrations. Office and shop workers had fled the eleven-storey building on two consecutive days. Scientists and building engineers in the city ruled out seismic activity or subsidence. The Mayor of Lille, Pierre Mauroy, ordered 300 Eurocity office workers to be relocated to hotels and closed most of the ground-level Eurolille shopping complex, which houses supermarkets and a sports shop.

The building, one of three glass and steel structures at Eurolille in the heart of the city, vibrated for several minutes between the third and seventh floors early one morning; the vibrations returned that afternoon. "The vibrations do not register on scientific instruments, but office workers say that their desks have moved and computer screens have gone haywire," a spokeswoman for the city hall said. "It seems that something in the building – a lift, perhaps – is emitting a frequency which the building itself is picking up and amplifying. It could take ages to track it down." No more vibrations have been reported, but monitoring continues.

PAPHOS

Two salesmen from an Israeli catering company were arrested on their way to a food fair in the southern Cypriot town of Paphos. An enormous plate of hummus strapped to the roof of their car had been mistaken for a spying gadget of some sort when the area was photographed by satellites. The salesmen were eventually released on bail of £12,500.

THE **PARANORMAL** WORLD

Top **10** Weird Events

1 PHANTOM LOLLIPOP LADY

NINE-YEAR-OLD Gemma Harris was playing near her Southend home when she saw the ghost of an elderly woman. "She was wearing a lollipop lady jacket with a big 'stop' badge on it," she said, "and she was very old with grey hair. I was a bit frightened." She appeared for a couple of minutes then turned white and moved away." Gemma's playmate, Claire Blanchard, also saw the spook. Both girls later drew near identical pictures of the spectre. Gemma's mother, Joanne Harris, said the girls were "petrified" and speculated that there had been some sort of traffic accident before their estate was built in 1995.

2 VAMPIRE MUMMIES

FOUR TINY mummies, said to be vampires by their owner, have been on display in a square in the centre of Jakarta, Indonesia. Hendra Hartanto says that the mummies were given to him by a group of psychics in eastern Java, and named them Jenglot, Betoro Katon, Begawan Kapiwiro and Bagawan Kapawiro. Jenglot, he said, was over 6,000 years old despite being only 6in (15cm) long. The mummies, he said, were kept alive by 1cc of human blood every 35 days. Hartanto tried to have them examined by the local hospital, but they refused - although they were keen to point out that the mummies were certainly not alive.

3 HOT PANTS

A SUPERMARKET worker was left with a 3in (7cm) scar on her bottom after her underwear "spontaneously combusted". Melanie Thompson said that her Marks and Spencer knickers caught fire while she was at the till of Hindley Co-op, Lancs. She ran to the loo, peeled off the smoking underwear, and doused it with water before returning to work. Marks and Spencer tested the knickers, but could find nothing out of the ordinary.

4 GHOSTS IN THE BELFRY

VILLAGERS AT Norrtälje in Sweden have acquired what appears to be a ghostly bell-ringer. Bells in their church have begun ringing in the middle of the night, with no obvious cause. Electricians examined the electronic bell-ringing system, but couldn't find anything wrong. In desperation, the power to the bells was turned off, but they continued to sound at around 2am. Experts have suggested that the ringing might be caused by interference from a nearby mobile phone antenna, but locals have objected, pointing out that it only ever occurs in the middle of the night.

THE SUN

⑤ SHE'S A FIRESTARTER

FIREMEN in Chiclayo in the north of Peru were called out twice in three days to mysterious fires in the same street. A three-year-old girl was rescued from her burning bedroom but investigators could find no obvious cause for the fire. Two days later, they put out a fire which had started in a bedroom where 13-year-old Giuliana Gutierrez Peralta was staying with a friend. The friend's father had told fire officials that during the night, Peralta had woken up with eyes that "seemed to shine in a variety of colours before turning glaring red." She started at the curtains, which caught fire. The local press demonised the girl, calling her *la niña del fuego* (fire girl) and *la hija del diablo* (the Devil's Daughter) and claiming that she could shoot fiery rays from her eyes "like Superman".

⑥ ALL SHOOK UP

A DUTCH Elvis impersonator claims that his plaster bust of the King has begun to cry. Toon Nieuwenhuisen, from the south-eastern town of Duerne, spotted moisture on the bust shortly before the August anniversary of Presley's death. He now invites the public into his home to view it in a spare bedroom full of candles and posters advertising his act. The 46-year-old performs as the Vegas-era Elvis and claims that the King's spirit possesses him whenever he sings.

⑦ WITHCRAFT TRIALS

GHANA'S WITCH villages have become the centre of a debate over how a modern government should deal with ancient beliefs. The villages form refuges for women accused of witchcraft. One such village is Gambaga, 30 miles (48km) from the nearest main road; over 100 accused women live there, in a cluster of mud-walled compounds on the edge of the town. They live in abject poverty, and are unable to leave without permission, but the villages at least offer them a haven from violent retribution. Most fear they would be killed if they returned to their homes.

⑧ VOODOO WARS

AN ANGRY crowd on the island of La Gonave, Haiti, burned a boat belonging to a ferry company which they suspected had used voodoo to sink a rival ferry. The crowd – mainly relatives of 200 people killed in an 1997 disaster – also attempted to lynch the company owner's wife as she tried to escape on a plane. Crying for revenge, the crowd chased her to the local police station where officers held them at bay. Her husband, Djo Jean-Joseph, had already fled, fearing for his life. The voodoo rumour apparently originated with the island's mayor.

⑨ CONSTABLE JESUS

A LANCASHIRE policeman has been nicknamed "Constable Jesus" by his colleagues due to his remarkable record of miraculous "resurrections". PC Stuart Janaway trained as a priest, and has been involved in at least 40 incidents involving apparent sudden deaths; in each case the victim has survived. On four occasions, paramedics at the scene were convinced of the patients' deaths. In one case, Janaway touched the wounds of a dying man who had been shot in the stomach and chest; he survived. Less supernaturally, he has also saved several people by massaging their hearts.

⑩ THE HOLE TRUTH

A ROMAN catholic priest in Antigua is said to have developed stigmata - mysterious "wounds" which appear in positions matching those traditionally associated with Christ's crucifixion. Wounds have appeared on his abdomen, his wrists and his ankles. Fr Gerard Critch, formerly of St John's Parish, Newfoundland, developed the wounds around Easter 1998, and has now been sent for specialist treatment in New York.

www.artoday.com

UFOs 1998
AMONG THE **SAUCERHEADS**

BRUCE WRIGHT sifts through the debris of another year in ufology.

HALE-BOPP: Comet of Doom

NASA

And what a strange and glorious time it was, filled with alarums and dubious claims and a dollop of millennial frenzy. The year opened beneath the baleful glare of Hale-Bopp, Comet of Doom (above). While H-B's milky smudge was something of a disappointment to a generation raised on Industrial Light and Magic, it served as a useful Rorschach blot for many of the more loosely configured minds on the saucer scene, which variously saw the comet as a harbinger of the New Age or merely the end of life on Earth. Cosmic muffin Courtney Brown of the Farsight Institute unveiled a photo, alas faked, of an H-B companion-object allegedly stuffed with extraterrestrials. His fellow "remote viewer" Ed Dames remotely saw the comet release a cylinder containing a pathogen that would

prediction bore fruit, as you may have noticed. But the claimants weathered their respective embarrassments rather better than did UFO old-timer Marshall Applewhite, who took his Nike-shod Heaven's Gate group comet-chasing with phenobarbital and vodka.

Just a few weeks before their departure came one of the most interesting UFO events in recent years, the "Phoenix Lights" case (bottom right). Hundreds of eyewitnesses described a V-shaped group of lights cruising slowly over and around Phoenix, Arizona for several hours on the night of 13 March 1997. As with all classic UFO cases, the explanation did not linger well on the palate. Thus it emerged that the lights were battlefield illumination flares dropped by a flight of A-10s as part of a training exercise; except that the sightings extended well beyond the military test range in question, and parachute flares are not usually given to flying in tight formation for hours on end. Meanwhile, a number of boringly respectable witnesses continue to insist that the lights they saw outlined a soundless, solid object that blotted out the stars. But their voices are lost in the desert wind.

As the Phoenix Lights twinkled out, momentum grew for the incredible Saucer Summer of 1997, when the fiftieth anniversaries of Kenneth Arnold's famous sighting and the so-called Roswell Incident merged into one of the great silly seasons of recent history. The festival peaked at July's "UFO Encounter" celebration in

saucerheads and other guileless party animals. An unveiling of genuine "alien metal fragments" proved an embarrassing fizzle, but on the other hand many T-shirts and refrigerator magnets were sold.

Publishers belched forth an unprecedented onslaught of UFO volumes, and everyone seemed to have at least one Roswell book in them, including the US government. America's Air Force echoed the comedic stylings of Operation Blue Book by proposing, in its *The Roswell Report: Case Closed*, that accounts of alien corpses in the 1940s could be explained by rubber test dummies parachuted over the desert in 1956. The time-traveling dummies of *Case Closed*, needless to say, failed to put much of a dent in the Roswell mythos, and another book gave it fresh impetus. *The Day After Roswell*, by retired military officer Philip J. Corso

CORSO: back-engineered

(below) and William Birnes, explained that saucer debris recovered at Roswell contributed to many post-1947 technological developments, due primarily to the vision and tireless patriotism of one Philip J. Corso. Most ufologists frowned on the work's discrepancies and technical illiteracy, but it sold briskly, which is, after all, what counts. Corso recently joined the Really Silent Majority, while his co-author has become publisher of America's *UFO Magazine*, and by a curious coincidence his book has begun receiving considerably better press in that journal.

1997 saw one of the most interesting revelations in the UFO

widely ignored. Historian Gerald K. Haines published a study in the CIA's unclassified journal *Studies of Intelligence* indicating that many of the often-derided Air Force "explanations" of UFO sightings in the 1950s and '60s were deliberate falsifications concocted to cover up sightings of top-secret military aircraft. Thus, for instance, some sightings of the high-altitude U-2 were dismissed as "ice crystals and temperature inversions". The implications of Haines' findings are uncomfortable for more than one faction in the UFO debate; apparently, a lot of those ritual Air Force invocations of Venus and whatnot, which sounded so much like feeble lies at the time, really were, despite the fortitude with which the skeptics of the day defended them.

Speaking of skeptics, a fascinating report of June 1998 prompted a burst of their rhetoric at its foam-flecked best. The Society for Scientific Exploration (SSE), a scientific organization devoted to the study of unexplained phenomena, produced a carefully worded study stating that the UFO phenomenon includes "intriguing and inexplicable observations," and that it "may be valuable to carefully evaluate UFO reports to extract information about unusual phenomena." Nothing too controversial there, you might think, but the funniest occult group of all, the Committee for the Scientific Investigation of Claims of the Paranormal (CSICOP), reacted with their customary inexplicable rage. CSICOP accused the SSE of harbouring "a hidden agenda" (gasp!) of "promoting fringe topics"; they also suggested that the report was timed to tie in with the release of *The X-Files* movie – which they hilariously denounced as "conspiracy

mongering", by the way – and that any investigation of UFOs might siphon funding from America's $35 billion science research budget. Ah. Yes.

Old-country readers can rest assured that their own isles continue to display a commendable knack for weirdness. I was delighted, for instance, to hear of a group of SAS troopers in South Armagh who encountered "four little grey men" who disappeared with a "brief flash of light", and of hovering brick-shaped objects sighted over Burton and South Derbyshire. Erratic lights, accompanied by explosions and a "crackling" noise, were observed up and down Scotland's east coast, and similar explosions rang out near the Butt of Lewis. In summer 1998, hundreds across England reported mysterious blue lights in the sky and, more entertainingly, a glowing "Z" shape seen in some areas for as long as 45 minutes. The UK military duly explained both the blue lights and the celestial mark of Zorro as meteors, but then they would, wouldn't they?

Also interesting was former Air Marshal Sir Peter Horsley's revealing account, first publicized in 1997, of his 1954 meeting with a telepathic alien named Janus. That Horsley later commanded the nation's nuclear arsenal caused many Britons to grow contemplative. In a more recent visitation, at least eight witnesses saw a brightly lit craft hovering near the Kent country home of former Home Secretary Michael Howard, to the profound embarrassment of the Conservative Party. No word on any messages delivered.

If Britain is holding its own in events, though, it seems decades behind in ufological practice, with players lacking the fervor needed for the sport. I do see promise, however, in one Max Burns, a UFO enthusiast

CRASH TEST: These are the Roswell aliens, dummy!

who devoted much of 1997 and 1998 to promoting the so-called "Sheffield event" of 24 March 1997, involving some unexplained sonic booms and triangle sightings over the Pennines. Author David Clarke investigated the incident and, to make a circuitous story short, it appears that Tornado aircraft involved in RAF training that evening may have gone supersonic in violation of military regulations. This dull explanation pales next to Burns' account, however, which involves a 300-foot (91m) extraterrestrial triangle buzzing rooftops near Sheffield before downing a Tornado, whose dead crewmen were whisked away by a secret government team. What Burns calls "damming evidence" (sic) does not appear conclusive – to the extent that I can decipher his unique prose. But I like his spirit, particularly when he dismisses Clarke and others as a "group of debunkers for and on behalf of the secret keepers", whatever that may mean. He's wasting his talent – he could move a hell of a lot of T-shirts in Roswell.

GHOSTLY GOINGS ON

Ghost hunters suffered a disappointment when one of the world's few scheduled ghosts failed to put in its expected appearence.

On 13 February 1748, the three-masted schooner Lady Luvibund (or Lovibund) set sail for Oporto in Portugal with a general cargo. Captain Simon Reed had just married and planned the voyage as both a business trip and honeymoon cruise. However, first mate John Rivers, who had been best man at the wedding, had a secret passion for the newlywed Annetta and was consumed with jealousy. It was

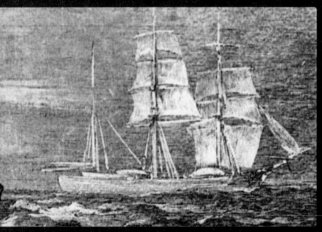

later reckoned that, as the Luvibund passed Deal in Kent, with the captain celebrating in his cabin with Annetta, her mother and some friends, Rivers took the helm and deliberately steered onto the Goodwin Sands, the nemesis of many ships over the centuries. The schooner broke up a mile north-east of the Goodwin lightship. There were no survivors. At the inquiry, the mate's mother told of her son's love and his vow to have revenge, even if it cost him his life. Offshore fishermen witnessed

the schooner's deliberate course to disaster.

On the 50th anniversary of the wreck, 13 February 1798, Captain James Westlake, master of the coaster Edenbridge, was almost rammed by a three-masted schooner as he skirted the Goodwins. He could hear female voices and laughter below deck. The authorities questioned the crew of a fishing vessel, who said the schooner had smashed into the Goodwin Sands and broken up; but when they hurried to investigate, there was no debris in the water and the sand bars were bare. The same scene was played out on 13 February 1848, witnessed by the crew of an American clipper and several locals, and on the 150th anniversary, witnessed from the shore. Narrators disagree on whether there was a sighting on 13 February 1948.

Some ghost hunters were expecting a real treat on the 250th anniversary – Friday, 13 February 1998. David Chamberlain crisscrossed the Goodwin Sands for six hours in his fishing smack, but saw nothing. On behalf of *Fortean Times*, Paul Sieveking and Jonathan Bryant drove down to Deal on the day and scanned the horizon without result. This was not unexpected; for one thing, the 250th anniversary was actually on Candlemas, 2 February 1998, as 2 September 1752 was followed by 14 September, when the Gregorian calendar replaced the Julian. Curiously, a map of wrecks on the wall of the café at the end of the pier, drawn up in 1977 by maritime disaster authority Richard Larn, marks the Luvibund wreck with the date 1746.

There are other problems. *Lloyd's Register of Wrecks*, held at the Guildhall

Library in London, makes no mention of the Luvibund nor does the *Gentleman's Magazine*. More troubling is the fact that the story has such a dubious pedigree. The earliest written reference found so far is the *Daily Chronicle* for 14 February 1924, which announced: "The anniversary of the ghostly visitation of the Lady Luvibund, sunk in the Goodwins in 1724, was marked last night by a terrific gale. There was at least one wreck, but from enquiries... the legendary apparition due every 50 years at midnight on February 13 was not seen."

The modern version of the tale, set in 1748, seems to have appeared first in *The Goodwin Sands* by former lightship crewman George Goldsmith-Carter, published in 1953. The author, now dead, told the fortean folklorist Michael Goss that he couldn't remember when or where he first heard the story. His version has much incidental detail, implying an omniscient narrator.

"Something must have snapped in John Rivers' brain, and walking casually aft he drew a heavy wooden belaying pin from the rack," he wrote. Then, according to Carter, Rivers crept up behind the helmsman and smashed him on the head before grabbing the helm and swinging it hard over to put the ship straight into the sands. "Above the din of a dying ship sounded the hideous cacophony of a madman's laughter." If the ship went down with all hands, how could this sequence of events be known?

Even if the Lady Luvibund had no basis in fact, we cannot rule out ghost ships on the Goodwins. George Carter himself had a strange experience on 1 February 1947 while serving on the North Goodwin lightship. Through a blizzard he and his shipmates saw a steamer heading for the Sands, followed by distress signals. They summoned the Ramsgate lifeboat, but no trace of a wreck could be found.

EMILY'S GHOST

Daniel Geraghty, 12, returning from a fishing trip near Barnsley in South Yorkshire, walked up Champney Hill, Silkstone Common, with his friend Darian Takeer. They heard footsteps walking up the grass verge at the side of the lane and a sound like someone sweeping up dead leaves. When they came to the top of the hill and looked down towards the wood, they saw a little girl dressed in "funny, old-fashioned clothes surrounded by a white mist." Petrified, Daniel and Darian walked down the lane and passed within 15ft (4.6m) of the figure, which stared at them before vanishing. They had also seen her the day before while walking Daniel's dog, and she had run off. Daniel's father Ken, 48, drew up a detailed picture of the girl from the boys' description (which Daniel is pictured holding). He delved into local records but came up with nothing – until his sketch and an account of the sighting appeared in the *Sheffield Star.* Jean Maloney, 68, thought the girl bore an eerie resemblance to her aunt, Emily Whitely, aged 11, who had died from head injuries in 1908 at nearby Champney Hill Farm when a shotgun being cleaned by farm labourer Lawrence Redfearn went off in the kitchen. Mrs Maloney produced a photograph of Emily aged eight (above centre). When Daniel saw

the picture he confirmed: "That's the girl I saw." The apparition was wearing a black choker, white lace gloves and a knee-length red velvet dress. She was carrying a stick or a broom. The photograph showed a girl wearing similar clothes, including matching choker. The hairstyles differed, but Mrs Maloney said that could be explained by the date of the photograph. "The lane where the boy spotted her is the place where she used to play as a child", she said. Ken Geraghty planned to have the lane blessed by a priest.

PRIESTS AND policemen are levying a "ghost tax" on drivers as they stop at toll booths in the eastern Indian state of Bihar. In return for cash, they guarantee that the spirits of drivers and animals killed in accidents will "spare" the travellers and ensure their safety.

A GHOST who smokes and tidies up seems to inhabit the vicarage of St Mark's Church, Cambridge. Her existence has been attested quite independently by three sceptical vicars in succession. The story featured briefly on ITV's *Signs and Wonders* at the end of 1997. Canon Bill Loveless noticed "a lot of crashing around at night", and his wife saw a young girl standing at the foot of the bed. Canon Philip Spence, his successor, was bemused by such odd occurrences – the forcing open of a rarely-used serving hatch, the arrangement of lace doilies under glass on a dressing table – that convinced him of a presence. "It was the very ordinariness of it all that convinced me," he said. Canon Christine Farrington, who has been vicar since March 1996, has also encountered the ethereal resident. Before she moved in, she saw "a forlorn young woman" standing at a window and has repeatedly caught a strong whiff of tobacco smoke.

LARGE CROWDS, closely watched by Burmese security forces, gathered regularly at a road junction in Rangoon (Yangon) after rumours circulated of a poltergeist terrorising a nearby block of flats, smashing glasses, cups and light bulbs. The intersection (in Myeinigone ward, Sanchaung township) was the scene of brutal police action against pro-democracy marchers in June 1987.

MEET THE

Don't fear the reaper? Well maybe you should. MARK CHORVINSKY speaks to people who've met the Grim Reaper and survived.

The Grim Reaper is a happening guy. In recent years he has had major roles in films and television, novels and rock songs. He has been death's poster boy for half a millennium. Until recently, though, students of the unexplained had no idea that the Reaper was anything but a symbol of death, a mythological figure. It is not often that a new subject is offered to the fortean field for consideration. I have been collecting accounts of Reaper sightings for some years and now have nearly one hundred cases in which someone encountered the Western personification of death. The description of the figure varies from case to case, but usually it is that of the classic Reaper – a black hooded robe, skeletal face and hands, often carrying a scythe. The sighting of this entity often precedes a death, sometimes by minutes. In other cases a day or more may pass before the death occurs. Sometimes the Reaper is encountered but is not associated with a death – or one that we know of.

It appears that there is a full blown Reaper phenomenon that somehow flew in under the fortean radar. How is it that fortean/paranormal investigators were not aware that such a phenomenon was occurring? There were some isolated Reaper cases spread out over a period of decades in the paranormal press, but they did not occur often enough to come to public attention. Also, there

I glanced to my right and there he was, standing by my side.

were no Reaper flaps, no media-driven "Reaper waves". A family member sees the Reaper at a relative's deathbed and never tells anyone until he writes to me about the experience. The growth of the phenomenon with respect to public consciousness was stunted, and without the benefit of newspaper clippings or articles in any scientific journals, there was little to alert fortean researchers and investigators to this very private phenomenon.

Now we know that the Angel of Death has been seen by the dying and their loved ones. As the cases come in and are analysed, we are struck by certain unexpected aspects of the mystery. Very often such phenomena conform to a cultural stereotype, and the Grim Reaper's is not too pretty. Yet paradoxically, some claim that the Reaper has been responsible for saving, rather than taking, lives. Instead of a horrific figure, he has been described as being patient, calming and even helpful. This is not what we would have predicted from a cultural standpoint, but as we learn more about the phenomenon and those who have had Reaper encounters, more of our questions should be answered.

I am not sure that there is a quintessential Reaper case, but that of A. L. of New York includes many of the classic elements and is a good introduction to the subject. In 1974, A. L. was living in an apartment in Yonkers, New York. It was about 10:15 pm and his children and wife were asleep. He

www.artlooby.com

REAPER

was in the living room sitting on the sofa when he had a strange feeling that someone was watching him. In his own words, A. L. describes his unexpected encounter with the personification of death:

"I slowly glanced to my right and there he was. Standing at my side, holding his scythe upright. He wore a black-hooded robe. His face was a gleaming white skull. He was just looking at me. I felt a cold chill go through me. Then fear came over me. I said out loud; 'Who sent you to me? Go back to where you came from.' With that command he glided slowly backward. He never turned his back to me. When he reached the front door he went right through it and he was gone. For a while I just stayed there thinking of what had happened. Why did he come to me and I'm still alive? I jumped up and ran to our bathroom thinking he could have come for someone else and I was too late. I called out to my wife and shook her. She was out cold with an empty bottle of pills on the bed. She had tried to take her life. I tried to wake her by walking her and slapping her. She was not responding. I ran to the telephone and called my sister who lived nearby. We drove her to the hospital and she was admitted. She was released a week later. We went on with our lives. I have learned that the Reaper is real."

I have interviewed A.L. at length. A corporate executive, he is the last person one might suspect would have such an experience. He does not want publicity and is afraid that if clients and colleagues knew of his Reaper encounter, he would lose some credibility.

The figure of the Reaper is common in our culture, from tattoos to T-shirts, from advertising to cartoons. But the majority of people I know who have encountered the Angel of Death never expected to see him – in fact, they generally did not even believe that such an entity existed or could exist.

If there is such a phenomenon as an entity that comes at the time of death, then we might expect to find that this occurs cross-culturally. Indeed, nearly every culture has a personification or god/goddess of Death. Some of the most fascinating cases are those described by doctors and nurses in India. In Hindu belief, Yama, the god of death, sends emissaries called Yamdoots to take the dying from our realm. It's believed that Yamdoots can take a number of different forms when they come to remove the prana (life force/breath) from the dying.

When he reached the door he went right through it and was gone.

Parapsychologists Karlis Osis and Erlendur Haraldsson collected the following account of a Yamdoot from an Indian doctor for their book *At the Hour of Death*. It reads like many Western Reaper accounts: "An educated lady in her sixties was admitted to the hospital for a checkup, there being no clear diagnosis. I examined her carefully, she had a slight fever but otherwise seemed normal. I told her; 'You simply have fever and after the checkup you can go home.' Some 20 minutes later she told visiting relatives that someone was whispering into her ear, 'Your time is over; come with me.' The relatives asked her who it was. 'Yamdoot,' she answered. The patient told this story two or three times. After that she was quiet and calm, became semi-conscious, and expired two or three hours later."

I can understand how one might see something odd under great stress, especially faced with one's own death or the death of a loved one. What could be more stressful? But what is the explanation for the following case?

C. L., of St. Charles, Missouri, is now 86. She was about 24 years old at

www.arttoday.com

the time of this incident. In 1936 she lived at Portage des Sioux, Missouri. Her son was ill at the Children's Hospital in St. Louis. As C. L. was on a streetcar, a couple got off, followed by a hooded, skeletal figure that ran around them, then continued onto the lawn and onto the porch of a house. C. L. had the impression that the conductor also saw this. The hooded figure was wearing long boards on its feet and stomped its feet loudly on the porch. There was a skull in the hood, its hands were bones and it was carrying a scythe. The streetcar started up. "It was like I was coming out of a daze," C. L. recalls. She had the feeling that the Reaper was there to take someone's life. The next day, on the way to the hospital, she watched for the house. When the trolley passed the home, she was startled to see that there was a black funeral wreath on the door.

Maybe every now and again someone dressed as the Grim Reaper takes a trolley and runs up to a house where someone is dying. I doubt it, though. Death is generally serious stuff. The only socially appropriate places to wear a Grim Reaper costume are at a '60s-style anti-war protest or a Halloween/Mardi Gras celebration. Although many of the cases I investigate do turn out to be hoaxes, throughout most of the C.L. investigation I felt that the hoax component was low to non-existent.

My thinking was that there was little chance of anyone dressing in a Reaper costume and hanging around hospital wards. While a number of otherwise sane individuals have been moved to dress up as Bigfoot and haunt their local forest, it takes a very warped sensibility to dress up as the personification of death and hang out where people are facing their own

www.arttoday.com

mortality. A case was recently brought to my attention in which a prankster dressed up as the Grim Reaper and was arrested after he was caught lurking around a nursing home in California. We now have our first known Reaper hoax. As for hoaxing by eyewitnesses, too many of the cases deal with the deaths or near-deaths of loved ones for the level to be high. These are very personal, often painful events for the witness to recall. Also, many of those who have seen the Reaper take their experience very seriously. This is especially true of those nurses and doctors who have seen the Reaper in the hospital rooms of those who were dying.

One of the most interesting of these encounters is described in a letter to me from a nurse: "I never thought there was such a thing as the Grim Reaper. I had always thought it was something someone thought up. I was working as a private duty nurse at the Diagnostic Hospital in Houston, Texas. It was an extremely hot day. I was running down the hall to get to my patient's room so I could relieve the nurse in charge. I had run past five rooms before I registered what I saw. I did not believe it! I went back down the hall and stopped at the room. On the bed was a little grey-haired lady propped up with pillows. Beside the bed stood this tall figure dressed in a monk's robe with its head covered. It looked up at me when I appeared in the door. His face was a skull with tiny red fires for eyes. His hands, skeletal, were folded over each other inside the dark sleeves. My impression was he was very patient, just waiting. When he looked at me I became almost frozen. I stepped back, turned and went down the hall to my patient's room. When the male nurse I shared my patient with saw me, he grabbed a blanket off the bed and wrapped it around me. I was freezing. He wrapped me in four blankets and put some hot chocolate in me. It took nearly two hours before I could even talk to him, and I told him what I saw. He said: 'Yes, the lady has been fighting death for over seven days.'" The patient died shortly thereafter, as in many of these cases.

What is the mechanism for such cases? Are they subjective or objective experiences? There are many variations on the basic Reaper sighting and the phenomenon is only beginning to define itself. I am currently continuing my research into the Reaper and am writing a book on the subject. If you have had a Reaper encounter or know of anyone who has, please contact this author at: *Strange Magazine, PO Box 2246, Rockville, MD 20847 USA* or email **strange1@strangemag.com**.

MIRACLES & WONDERS

The power of faith or divine intervention? No, we don't know either, but there's been no shortage of miracles to keep us wondering.

AUDREY SANTO

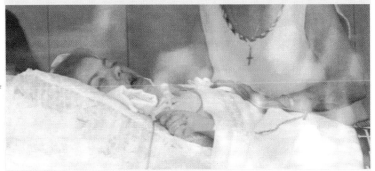

 13-year-old girl in Springfield, Massachusetts, is under consideration for canonisation by the Church. Audrey Santo went into a coma after an accident when she was three. Doctors say she is in a permanent vegetative state. She breathes on her own, her fingers twitch and her eyes move, but they remain unfocused. She bears the stigmata of the crucifixion: her hands, feet and side ooze blood and the wounds from the crown of thorns appear periodically on her forehead. Every week, crucifixes, Virgin Mary statues and other artefacts in her room secrete oil, which is collected and used to anoint those seeking a cure.

According to the Rev. George Joyce, spiritual advisor to Audrey's parents, all the child's miraculous cures have been independently investigated and video-taped. It is said the lame have walked and the blind have seen. A rash, similar to ones seen on cancer victims during chemotherapy, once appeared on Audrey's legs for a month. As it faded, a group of mothers who had been praying to her because their children had cancer reported that the children were cured. Sensitive to accusations of trickery, Audrey's parents do not solicit payment, though visitors often donate to the Rev Joyce's Church of Our Lady of Hope.

DANIELLE O'CONNOR

 anielle O'Connor, a six-year-old from Motherwell in Lanarkshire is claimed to have recovered from an incredibly rare genetic condition after her parents had her blessed with relics of the Italian stigmatic priest Padre Pio. Danielle was born with a condition called 21-chromosome deficiency, which normally causes stunted growth and severe mental handicap; it also drastically shortens life expectancy. However, when Danielle was two years old, her parents held a bandage from Pio's wounds and a set of his rosary beads over her head during a private blessing ceremony. Since then, her parents Frank and Maureen say she has continued to develop reasonably normally; she does not attend a special school, and apparently has a high reading ability for her age. Frank and Maureen are keen to attribute these effects to Pio: "I am convinced she has been cured by the blessing," her mother said. Her case records were forwarded to the Vatican as part of an ongoing campaign to have Pio canonised; perhaps they worked, for Pio was beatified – a preliminary step toward sainthood – in 1997.

CROATIAN SHEPHERD BOYS

 housands of people, pious or curious, have been streaming to Grab in Bosnia-Herzegovina, 60 miles (96km) southwest of Sarajevo, drawn by media reports of an apparition of Jesus that two Croat shepherd boys claim to have seen on a window shutter in a ruined house on 4 January.

"We heard some noise and a little cloud of fog appeared," said Ivan Grbavac, aged nine. "On the shutter on the window, we saw a head." They ran away screaming after which Ivan's mother came out to see what was going on. "It was Him on the window – Jesus Christ – and I crossed myself," said Desanka Grbavac.

Most of the visitors are from Bosnia and Croatia, but they are also bussing in from Germany and Italy. "I don't know whether this is for real or not, but the fact is that I can see a figure and a crucifix," said a second-time visitor who identified himself only as Zoran.

If the interest keeps up in spite of the Church's silence, then poverty may no longer be a way of life in Grab. Its 1,000 residents need only look to nearby Medjugorje, where fortunes soared after a group of children reported seeing the Virgin Mary 17 years ago. Even though Bishop Zanic of nearby Mostar is in open feud with the Franciscan Friars who run the Medjugorje operation, millions of pilgrims have made the once-poor village one of Europe's most-visited shrines. Villas with tennis courts and pools, mansions and motels have replaced old stone shacks and cottages.

THE HIEROPHANT PREDICTS

PHIL BOND

THE FUTURE, AS THE GREAT PROPHET CRISWELL MEMORABLY ANNOUNCED, IS WHERE WE ARE GOING TO SPEND THE REST OF OUR LIVES. *FORTEAN TIMES'* RESIDENT ALL-SEEING ASCENDED MASTER AND GOSSIP COLUMNIST THE HIEROPHANT PRESENTS HIS GUIDE TO THE INSIDE SKINNY ON NEXT YEAR'S BIG NEWS STORIES...

JANUARY

A new book appears arguing that humans alone could not have created the vast piles of ancient astronaut books left lying around after the January sales. The author even claims that some of the books exhibit clear signs of somehow having been deliberately constructed by an incomprehensible intelligence. A search is organised for a vast stash of ancient astronaut literature thought to be buried on the Giza Plateau. A sequel soon follows, revealing that – by careful analysis of mystical geometry and a *London A-Z* – it can be demonstrated that Jesus is buried under a New Age shop on Greenwich High Street.

FEBRUARY

There is alarm when NASA releases the news that computer analysis of satellite photographs has revealed that Milton Keynes, Hull and the entire county of Merseyside are, in fact, chance effects of shadow and sunlight moving over natural weathering patterns. Calm is soon restored when it is realised that nobody actually cares.

This year's first photos appear purporting to show the Loch Ness Monster. Unusually, the Monster is shown buying 12 cans of Kestrel and 40 Rothmans in an Edinburgh off-licence prior to a Hearts – Hamilton Academicals friendly; "a wake", say the skeptics.

MARCH

Several American radio shows present interviews with an alleged former NASA employee who complains that the Antediluvian Order of Buffaloes are using their influence with the agency to suppress information regarding strange tower-like structures, spaceship-like objects and so-called "rocket launchers" in the area of Cape Canaveral, Florida. According to the former space scientist, the authorities fear the impact on human society of proof of sentient life in Florida.

APRIL

Fortean Times' UnConvention '99 takes place in London. The normally sober proceedings are somewhat disrupted by the Centre for Fortean Zoology's controversial decision to bring along a live panther to show would-be ABC spotters just what it is they're looking for. Several of the slower attendees meet with unfortunate ends over the weekend after the panther takes up residence in the venue's crawlspaces. There is a hasty re-think of UnCon 2000's mooted theme, "Vampires, Werewolves, and Enormous Killer Robots With Chainsaws".

MAY

Moslem scholars are thrown into chaos when no holy fruit, vegetables or even pulses are discovered anywhere for the whole month. "It's terrifying," reports one Sufi sage, "we haven't had so much as a verse from the *Hadith of Muhammed Ali* on a parsnip, never mind the Holy Name in an aubergine." Opinion is divided as to the precise meaning of this portent.

There is turmoil in the world of astrology when every Cancer in Britain buys a winning ticket for the National Lottery. Mystic Meg goes into hiding.

JUNE

There is a brief flurry of excitement when a number of strange, stinking hairy humanoids are sighted in woodlands near Seattle, Washington. Sadly, the discovery of high amounts of coffee, heroin and Cheetos in the creatures' faeces demonstrates that they are merely former members of the grunge bands nobody cares about any more. Several are persuaded to form a Nirvana tribute band which tours the US to no particular acclaim.

The latest conspiracy tome arrives from America, claiming that the world's drug trade is in fact controlled by the gimpylooking bloke from the *Mr Muscle* adverts and the surviving cast members of *Dad's Army*. "The facts speak for themselves," says the author, shortly before his bizarre suicide by drowning, poisoning, hanging (twice), shooting and pulling all his fingernails out with pliers.

JULY

The annual crop circle mania reaches its height when an intricate halftone image of arch skeptic James Randi is found in a field near Stonehenge. Remarkably, intensive dowsing and dreamwork reveals that the formation's site is one of the few in Wiltshire with no mystical resonances of any sort whatsoever. Believers take this as dreadfully significant. Within the week, a further pictogram appears nearby, this time taking the form of a communication from an alien intelligence, claiming that the Randi image was the work of hoaxers from Proxima Centuri.

52nd anniversary of the Roswell crash goes curiously unmarked by world's news media.

AUGUST

This year's oddball UFO cult appears. Calling themselves the Brotherhood of Michael, and taking their lead from reports of heavy UFO activity in the region of former Tory cabinet minister Michael Howard's home, they reportedly belive that motherships from a far-distant world will arrive some time in December 1999. The faithful will be taken aboard the spaceships and travel to the alien homeworld, a land of peace, wisdom and plenty, where they will be subjected to a rigorous 18-month immigration check to ensure that their claims for asylum from Earth are in fact valid. They will then be deported back to Earth. Membership is reassuringly small.

The lost sunken land of Lyonesse, long reputed to lie off the Cornish coast, reappears during this month's total solar eclipse. Sadly, its reappearence is at the cost of Cornwall, which sinks under the weight of the millions of gathered eclipse-watchers. Popular opinion holds that this is a fair trade-off.

SEPTEMBER

The slew of fortean-themed media reaches its logical conclusion with the appearence of Andrew Lloyd Webber's musical version of Charles Fort's *Book of the Damned*. Lord Lloyd Webber's music accompanies Richard Stilgoe's lyical interpretation of Fort's ideosyncratic philosophy. Opening number "Mad Fishmongers and Flying Frogs" is a minor hit and soon becomes a karaoke favourite, although the Reverend Lionel Fanthorpe's performance as Fort raises a few eyebrows, not least because of his insistence on performing astride his beloved Harley-Davidson. At the cinema, meanwhile, it becomes clear that the ideas for good fortean movies are running out when three major studios announce that their summer blockbusters will be all-action adventures about entombed toads.

OCTOBER

The famous Patterson bigfoot film is analysed using the very latest digital image and video processing techniques, with surprising results. After consultation with several eminent biologists, cryptozoologists, anatomists and special-effects experts, a statement is issued confirming that the creature in the film is indeed an unknown hominid, but an unknown hominid wearing a crappy ape suit. "The implications are incredible," say the analysts. "Not only does this imply intelligence on the part of Bigfoot, but also an unusually highly-developed sense of humour, for a primate. Sadly, his needlework appears less well developed."

NOVEMBER

Conspiracy theorists and ufologists rejoice (briefly) when the US Air Force and NASA admit that, yes, they have been holding on to captured aliens for the last forty or fifty years. The celebrations are short-lived when they add that the reason they haven't released the news previously is that the creatures are simply depressingly stupid, and they didn't feel the world was quite ready for this momentous news. Most of the creatures' time on earth, it is revealed, has been spent in drinking beer, making fart noises with their armpits and throwing spitballs at each other.

DECEMBER

According to Dr Ernesto Moshe Montgomery of the Beta Israel Temple in Los Angeles, Shirley MacLaine is due to be a catalyst in bringing peace to the world by the year 2000*. This month will bring her last chance when a nuclear war almost breaks out between two American militia groups. The One True Christian White Nation Of The Holy Blood Of The Aryan Christ and the One True Christian White Nation Of The Holy Blood Of The Aryan Christ (Non-Subscribing) come to blows over precisely where in the Revelation of St John the names of Bill and Hilary Clinton are to be found. Although NORAD briefly registers DEFCON 1, the situation is defused when the two sort out their differences and resolve to destroy the Zionist heretics of the True White Christian Nation Of The Holy Blood Of The Aryan Christ.

And there we have to leave 1999. I'd dearly love to pass on news of 2000, but things seem a little opaque after January 1st – all that comes through my scrying devices is screaming...

The Hierophant opens his files on all the gossip and sleaze of the paranomal world every month in *Fortean Times*.

*This is true.

FAIRYSALE: A TRUE STORY

Over eighty years ago two young girls fooled the world's greatest minds with their faked fairy photographs. This year a little bit of fortean history went on sale. CHRISTINE WOOD reports.

LISTEN TO THE BAND: Frances and the fairy folk.

Some forteana is timeless. Generations of children are raised on ghosts, monsters and, of course, fairies. Perhaps this explains why, more than 80 years after the first pictures were taken, the Cottingley Fairies have never lost their charm.

Recently there has been a resurgence of interest in these particular fairy-folk. The story has formed the basis for one film *Fairytale - A True Story* and acted as a catalyst in another – *Photographing Fairies* – and there have been two high-profile auctions of Cottingley memorabilia.

The story began in 1917 when Elsie Wright and her cousin Frances borrowed a camera from Elsie's father and photographed fairies near their home in Cottingley, West Yorkshire. The pictures soon came to the attention of Sir Arthur Conan Doyle, who believed the pictures to show evidence of real fairies. It was Conan Doyle who released these stunning images to the public in 1920 and who immortalised their story in his 1922 book *The Coming of the Fairies*.

Both Elsie and Frances maintained that the pictures were real throughout the various technical tests performed during the 1920s. It was not until 18th February 1983 that Elsie admitted to the hoax. She made her belated confession because, she said, she did not want her grandchildren to think that she was a 'nutter'. Frances confessed soon after. Both women insisted, however, that one photograph, 'Fairies And Their Sunbath', was not a fake.

Elsie had begun to put her past behind her some years before. In 1972 she sold both her father's Standard Midg Falling Plate camera, used for the original fairy pictures, and the Cameo Plate camera, supplied by Gardner for further pictures, along with five original prints at auction. The funds raised were apparently needed to buy a new lawnmower. The pieces were bought by Sydney J. Robinson, a Conan Doyle expert, who turned to Geoffrey Crawley in an attempt to solve the mystery. Robinson eventually passed on his collection to Crawley, who had begun to amass a great deal of fairy memorabilia.

Crawley sent this collection, in three lots, for auction at Christie's on 19th March 1998.

The first lot included a very rare copy of *Princess Mary's Gift Book* and two silver-gelatin prints of 'Elsie and the Gnome' and 'Frances and the Fairies.' They were bought by Ms Ginger Gilmore, an American living in East Sussex, for £368. Ms Gilmore bought the lot because she "believes in the magic of fairies" and also wanted them for her children.

Lot number two was bought by another American, this time a private collector living in London. John Arieta became fascinated with the story of the Cottingley fairies after seeing the photographs in the British Museum's *Fake!* exhibition in the 1980s. He paid £1,092 for three silver-gelatin prints, two cut-film negatives, an undated newspaper clipping about the story and a letter from Gardner to Mrs Wright. This letter gives details of the independent examinations performed by "one of the best experts in London" and Gardner writes... "We want to learn something further about the fairy world and the very best way will be by photographs, if only we can obtain them."

Neither lot was given a reserve price, indicating that they were not expected to fetch in excess of £200.

The final lot included both the Midg and Cameo cameras, five gelatin-silver prints, a pre-retouch copy of one of the photographs, three watercolour sketches of fairies by Elsie, a nine-page letter from Elsie to Crawley, a first edition copy of Doyle's *The Coming of the Fairies* and Crawley's *The Astonishing Affair of the Cottingley Fairies*, originally published in the *British Journal of Photography*. The reserve price for all these items was set at only £500-£800.

On hearing about the impending sale, *Amateur Photographer* magazine and Bradford's *Telegraph and Argus* newspaper decided to band together and form a campaign to keep the cameras in Britain. It was feared that the pieces would be taken out of the country by an American collector. In all, the campaign managed to raise £13,000, £2,500 of which was donated by members of the public. The rest of the money was donated by Olympus, Canon and photographic retailers Jessops. Negotiations with Crawley followed and it was agreed that the cameras should be housed in the National Museum of Photography, Film and Television in Bradford. It is generally thought that Crawley wanted the cameras to stay in Britain as much as anyone else did.

The cameras were presented to the museum in a civil ceremony attended by around 2,000 people on 26th June 1998. They are currently housed in the foyer of the museum's Pictureville cinema until renovations to the NMPFT are completed in 2000. They will then be put on permanent display. On 12th September 1998 the cameras returned home to Cottingley where they were displayed in the Town Hall for the day

at the request of local residents.

It later emerged that Mel Gibson offered £20,000 for the cameras, unfortunately after the museum deal had been struck. Obviously sincerely interested, Gibson agreed to appear in the uncredited, non-speaking role of Frances' father in *Fairytale - A True Story* and was recently quoted as saying:

"One of the books my wife had when I first met her was about the little girls who photographed fairies out in the glen in 1917... How could the girls have done it with the equipment they had then? I just always thought it was an intriguing magic story."

On 16th July 1998 a second sale of fairy memorabilia took place, this time at Sotheby's. The owner of this collection was Frances' daughter, Christine Lynch. All three lots were bought by one person, a London bookseller who apparently plans to sell the items on.

Simon Finch purchased, amongst other items, a set of Cottingley fairies photographs, sent to Frances by Sir Arthur Conan Doyle, for £8,050.

Also at auction was another first edition copy of *The Coming of the Fairies*. Rather more special than the previous copy sold, this one was inscribed to Frances Griffiths "with kind regards from Arthur Conan Doyle, Sept 7 1922" and also included the signature of her cousin and fellow faker, Elsie. The reserve price for Frances' book was £3,500. The final price paid was £8,970.

Surprisingly one of the most important lots raised the least money. Thirty-seven glass lantern slides in their original box carrying the name and address of Gardner and which he used in his lectures, failed marginally to reach their reserve price of £5,000.

Along with the slides, the lot included the December 1920 and January 1921 editions of *The Strand* magazine, which reportedly sold out within three days and included articles by Conan Doyle and Gardner on the fairies, along with 31 positive prints which featured shots of the girls taken in rural surroundings.

This brought the final total paid by Simon Finch to £21,620, almost double pre-sale expectations.

The reason for this spate of sales seems obvious, but possibly slightly cynical. It is believed that Christine Lynch's publishing company will soon produce a book on the subject. Crawley's sale has also been described as 'good timing', if he did not sell the items now he would potentially never have the market to do so again. The recent films based upon the story have generated more public interest in the tale than has been seen since the confessions of the early 1980s. It is the obvious time to sell.

It is comforting to know that these pieces of childhood history will no longer be locked away and future generations will be able to enjoy the very machines that once photographed 'real-life' fairies.

TURNING HEADS: Elsie watches the fairies.

GHOSTS I HAVE KNOWN

ANDREW GREEN recalls some of the close encounters and near misses he's had over a lifetime spent in search of spooks

BORLEY CHURCH: Opposite the site of the legendary rectory.

Have I really known any? As a professional investigator, I feel it wise to establish that in over 40 years of research, I think that I have only had the doubtful pleasure of witnessing one genuine phantom, apparition, ghost, spectre or whatever, and that was of a dog that had been seen in the same bedroom by six other guests, in my uncle's home in Devon, within the previous 12 months.

The incident that created my initial interest in the 'unknown' was taking a photograph of an empty building in 1944 in which, according to police records, 20 suicides and a murder had occurred between 1883 and 1934. The image of a young girl of "about 12 years of age was clearly visible looking out from one of the upper windows", according to the chemist who processed the film,

though the house was locked and had been derelict for some 10 years. The photo was later used as the dust cover for my first major book,.*Our Haunted Kingdom*, but still provokes comments like "who is the tall man with a top hat behind the girl?", or "what about the little old woman standing beside the poor wee soul?" Someone, perhaps envious of not having taken the photo himself, huffed "it's a reflection", to which I have to reply, "from where?", as the nearest building to provide one is over 30 miles away.

Having formed a small research group a short while later, I was asked by the owner of a local hotel to organise an investigation into the haunting of the premises, by, believe it or not, "a little green man who runs up and down the stairs, but only at weekends. He has been seen quite often by a couple of regular guests." It was easy to establish that the "regular guests" would arrive with a crate of whisky on Friday night, direct from Belfast, and depart somewhat painfully on the Monday morning, leaving the empty bottles for "the spirit collector". The hotelier had, unbeknown to us, told the local press that the "haunting was waiting to be confirmed by a specialist group of top line scientists," in order, she admitted, to charge extra for seeing the spectral visitor.

Another rather mystifying incident occurred during a weekend visit to the site of the famous Borley rectory. When – at two in the morning – a colleague and I were strolling past the abandoned Rectory garden, we were subjected to an unearthly, spine-chilling scream from a late-night worker cycling past us. He returned seconds later to repeat the

performance and disappeared into the courtyard of the former coach house. We were later assured by the owner of the cottage that he knew nothing about the traveller and the only bicycle he had was a very badly rusted machine, leaning against the outside wall. When we looked at our rather outlandish clothing however, we both realised the probable cause for the scream. With my dark trousers and my colleague's dark top, we would have appeared in the moonlight as a weird headless and legless torso standing next to a man with legs but no body.

Earlier my associate had become rather upset with me because I was totally unable to see "the shimmering figure of the ghostly nun, approaching from about 60 feet away." All I could recognise was a cloud of midges following the track of an underground stream, and as for the "horrifying and soul shivering moan" heard in Borley church, I disappointed him and his wife by establishing the sound was that of a cow rubbing itself against the outside wall near the altar.

My outstanding failure as a "secular exorcist" – a term provided by the BBC – was when I was required to assist an elderly gentleman of 97 suffering, it was stated, from the attentions of a female poltergeist who would interfere with him at night. So

GHOST RIDE: Blue Bell Hill, Kent – home to a phantom h

HOLY GHOST: The spectre of St Thierot is said to be visible on the left side of this photo, taken in May 1984 at Fordeil Castle in Fife.

SPOOKY PEW: The photographer claimed there was no-one in front of the camera when he took this snap in Eastry Church, Kent,. But note the open pew door.

disturbing was the effect that he had to sleep with an open umbrella between his legs – a succubus case in the 20th century no less! "The vicar is no good," I was told by the victim, "he's religious and can't understand. But the nurses at the hospital could see her sitting on my shoulder most times. I'm surprised you are unable to see her." I was unable to eradicate the problem and had to leave it in the hands of the sufferer's 96-year-old house-keeper whom he admitted to "desiring".

Hitting the news headlines, not just in the UK, but in Europe, Australia, and America, including Mexico, was the report in 1997 that "a specialist ghost-hunter" – this term makes me cringe, I do not 'hunt' or 'bust' ghosts – had been called upon to investigate the alleged haunting of the Royal Albert Hall. The problem was caused by an executive member of the security staff seeing the figures of two young women "wearing old fashioned clothing" approaching the entrance to the kitchen, below the area accessible to the public, and on being challenged, seeing them turn round and "just fade away". Research suggests that they were the shades of two 'residents' of the 19th century brothel that then existed in Kensington Gore, the original site of the hall, but their appearance caused no suggestion of hysteria or fright, merely amusement and puzzlement. There were, nevertheless, other experiences that could have been cause for concern. A bell had sounded near Gateway 6 under mysterious circumstances, internal doors had slammed inexplicably and an "uncomfortable feeling of being watched and being gently pushed by an unseen force" was experienced by another member, in what was originally 'The Garden Room'. At this time, a corridor circled the Willis Organ on the top floor, in which old stairways were being removed to make way for the

THE GARDEN ROOM GHOST: Strange goings on behind the Willis organ of the Royal Albert Hall.

installation of lifts. It was most certainly a weird location, especially as it affected my thermometer, which registered a sudden and unexplainable increase of 10 degrees, from 71° to 81°, within a few seconds of arrival. Having walked round the auditorium tape recording my impressions and giving a general commentary, I was more than a little puzzled, playing the tape back, to hear that the amount of static, when near the organ, was so intense that I was unable to make any sense of the distorted sound. Such spectral static certainly seems to produce problems when using any form of electrical equipment.

What to me was a really interesting and informative investigation resulted from a request of a former staff member of the Old Bailey, who claimed that he had experienced inexplicable phenomena in the building and asked for clarification. The two areas of the 'haunting', which consisted of the sound of footsteps, adjoined the old Roman wall, past which condemned prisoners would be taken, and the underground area housing the massive central heating system.

Two years ago I was involved in arranging an official ghost tour in the Southeast of England for an American leisure organisation. One of the reputedly haunted sites in which they wanted to carry out a 'night vigil' was Herstmonceux Castle in Sussex, owned by the Queen's University of Kingston, Ontario, and used as a study and conference centre. For decades a claim has been made that the castle is affected by the sound of a phantom headless drummer, which was probably the activity of a gardener employed to frighten the inmates and to conceal the operations of

smugglers who were, unbeknown to the owners in the 18th century, using the castle for "nefarious purposes".

The visitors were duly accommodated in 'The Drummers Room' with the agreement that I would collect them at 10 in the morning, following their 'full English breakfast'. On arrival, shortly before the pick-up time, I chatted to the receptionist about the visitors and their hopes and learnt, with some astonishment, that while preparing a buffet for some visiting lecturers on the ground floor, immediately below the Drummers Room, she had actually heard the sound of "the ghost". "He was drumming for quite a few seconds," I was told, "softly at first and rather slowly, but then quite loudly. It didn't worry me, for I have heard it once before

The "evil spirit" was a reflection from a poster

when we had overseas visitors staying in that room." I asked the time of the incident and the young lady said that it was "about 11.30pm". A few minutes later my 'guests' came down the stairs, looking somewhat bedraggled, but on enquiring as to any experiences, I was assured that they had none, though they thoroughly enjoyed the breakfast. "What time did you manage to get to sleep?" The couple looked at each other. The man blushed slightly and said, "about 11.45, I guess". I felt that the drumming had been satisfactorily accounted for – at least on that occasion.

Called upon by a Race Relations Board in the 1980s, I spent many hours trying to explain and comfort a victim who was convinced that his house was 'possessed', into accepting that the "frightening moans and cries" that he and his family heard, were due to a faulty water cistern installation, and that the 8ft (2.4m) tall "ghost" that he saw early one morning, could not really have been responsible for the pools of water in the bathroom.

The "evil spirit" was a reflection from a poster in a shop window opposite the house.

A new twist in the world of ghosts is the current trend towards obtaining compensation for anything and everything. During the summer of 1998 a family sued two sisters for selling their home to them without disclosing that it was 'haunted'. Efforts by a local vicar to eradicate, not exorcise, the invisible spectre – as rather expected – only worsened the incidents of poltergeist activity, arising probably from the three children of the new owners and the considerable stress arising from the move. Last year a new purchaser of a home in the Midlands sued the previous owner for exactly the opposite reason. There were not the number of ghosts in the property that he had been lead to believe.

Such phantoms are liable, it seems, to appear sometimes at the most inconvenient times and places. At least three public toilets, to my knowledge, house potentially embarassing spectres. There are a large number of haunted pubs and hotels and some are affected by bottom-pinching phantoms. Let's hope that one day we'll see a compensation plea from a victim willing to be examined by a court of law.

HAUNTED HOUSE: The picture that started it all for Andrew Green.

LOSING OUR **RELIGION**

Religious apparitions, manifestations and phenomena of all sorts seem to be increasing in frequency every year. Whether this is just pre-millennial hysteria remains to be seen; in the meantime, here's a selection of some of the best religious stories of the last year.

PATRON SAINT OF REAL ESTATE

Religious supply stores in the USA sell more than two million statues of Saint Joseph every year. The statues are bought by home-sellers for burial in the yard, in the belief that the patron saint of the home can expedite a speedy sale.

The belief is a persistent one, reinforced by tales such as this one. Norma Deckley's four-bedroom house in Phoenix, Arizona, had been on the market for four months, and no-one showed any interest. As she had already bought a new house and was paying for both, she was open to any suggestions. Several Catholic friends told her to buy a statue of St Joseph and bury it upside-down in her yard. "I thought it was just baloney," she said, "but my husband buried it on Thursday and we sold it that weekend."

Realestate agent Judy Nelson is another convert. "I got turned on to this several years ago by a client whose house we just couldn't seem to sell," she said. "So we went and bought four St Joseph statues and had them blessed by a priest." After the statues were buried, the house sold immediately. She dug up the statues and has used them successfully for the past ten years.

Inevitably – this being America – there are now St Joseph kits, which sell for $8.95 (£5.60) and include a prayer card and an introduction to the use of the St Joseph home-sale practice. These were first marketed in 1994 by Jerry Micklewright, a certified public accountant in Cary, Illinois. In that year, he made 8,000 statues; last year, he sold 47,000 and this year hopes he can make it to 75,000.

Micklewright has his own miraculous anecdote. Back in 1980 or 1981, he had been in the same position as Norma Deckley: he had bought a house but couldn't offload the old one. He then recalled that his father had told him years before that if he had trouble selling a house, he should say a prayer and bury a St Joseph statue. This he did and the house went for the asking price the very next day. All hail St Joseph!

VIRGIN VISITS EGYPT

FIRST CAME flashes of red light around the steeple of the Virgin Mary church in Shentena al Hagar, a small Egyptian village near Menufiya, 44 miles (70km) north of Cairo. Then silver-white doves flew overhead. Finally the Virgin Mary herself, in white robe and blue veil, alighted atop the steeple – a vision to the faithful. Within a month of this appearance, 150,000 pilgrims from around Egypt and beyond had come to see the vision, according to the parish priest, Father Youanis Rateb Abdel-Mour. It was implied that the vision could be seen every night. Father Wisa Baqui from a neighbouring village described how the Virgin "appeared on the church tower with two angels by her side and began moving and blessing the people".

The sightings were confirmed by Bishop Benjamin of Menufiya. "I saw her three times. She appeared in very bright circles of light. The third time I saw her transforming into a huge silver dove piercing the sky. After sending two committees to investigate, the patriarch of Egypt's Coptic Church, Pope Shenouda III, issued a statement saying an "unnatural light" had appeared in the church. He hailed it as "a spiritual appearance" but did not refer to the Virgin Mary.

SAVED BY THE BOOK

PROVIDENCE EMPLOYED the classic prayer-book defence in New Orleans. Two nuns were chatting to a policeman in front of the Sisters Servants of Mary convent when a fleeing armed robber fired at them several times, apparently thinking the policeman was going to give chase. A bullet passed through the prayer book of one of the women, then hit her in the hip. The 38-year-old woman was treated at a hospital and released. The gunman escaped, but Sgt Marion Defillo said police were searching for a man wanted in connection with at least 16 armed robberies of convenience stores.

CROP**CIRCLE**GALLERY

Ten years on we're still as enchanted as ever by these cereal enigmas. 1998 saw a bumper harvest in England, and circles also appeared as far afield as the USA, Hungary and the Czech Republic. Here's our pick of the crop.
Photos by STEPHEN ALEXANDER

DADFORD, Bucks, UK (4/7/98) *crop: Wheat*

EAST KENNET, Wilts, UK (3/5/98) *crop: Oil Seed Rape*

BECKHAMPTON, Wilts, UK (20/6/98) *crop: Wheat*

WEST WOODS, Wilts, UK (11/7/98) *crop: Wheat*

THE SANCTUARY, Wilts, UK (19/8/98) *crop: Wheat*

BECKHAMPTON, Wilts, UK (21/7/98) *crop: Wheat*

BECKHAMPTON, Wilts, UK (8/8/98) *crop: Wheat*

FAREHAM, Hants, UK (11/7/98) *crop: Wheat*

A **BEGINNER'S** GUIDE TO
CROP**CIRCLE** MAKING

You don't need to be an alien, a plasma vortex or even a higher intelligence to make a crop circle. ROB IRVING lays it all out in the open.

Follow this step by step guide and, with a little practice, you too will be producing genuine, dowsable, scientifically unhoaxable circles and patterns.

Disclaimer:
Trespassing and damaging crops are criminal offences. If you do plan to make crop circles, ask the farmer's permission first.

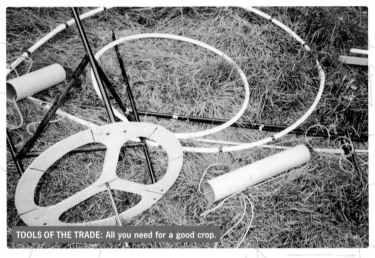
TOOLS OF THE TRADE: All you need for a good crop.

THE CANVAS:

While most crops, from spinach to rice, have played host to circles, three are preferred: oil-seed rape in April through May, barley in May and early June, and wheat from mid-June until August.

EQUIPMENT:

The tools you will need are relatively unsophisticated and can be obtained easily.

• 30m (99ft) surveyor's tape – *preferable to string which tangles easily.*

• 1.2m (3.9ft) plank with a rope attached to each end, forming a bridle – *this is commonly known as a stalk-stomper. Size can vary to taste. One group of circlemakers, known for their large appetite, wield the legendary 'Robo-stomper' – a veritable 3m (9.9ft) monster assembled in situ.*

• Plastic garden roller – *for that smoother finish.*

• Luminous watch – *summer nights can be surprisingly brief.*

• Dowsing rods – *preferably copper, and purchased from an expensive New Age shop, though in an emergency a couple of bent coat-hangers will do.*

PREPARATION:

1. Choose a location in daylight. A field rising up from the road, or a natural amphitheatre, make perfect circles sites.

2. Plan your design carefully, bearing in mind that a diagram may not be easily visible in the dark. Think big: a small pattern is easily swamped by a large field, and can appear amateurish and fake.

3. If possible, establish earth energies by dowsing the field beforehand. Patterns located on leys will satisfy later tests for genuineness, while aiding healings, orgone accumulation, angelic visions, benign abduction experiences and generating feelings of general well-being. Warning: Contra-directional energy flows may result in headaches, nausea, temporary paralysis, aching joints, sore, runny or bleeding orifices, mental illness, Deadly Orgone Radiation (DOR), demonic visions, negative abduction scenarios and general disillusionment.

4. Once location and design have been decided, retire to a pub and wait for darkness. If you are in a circles-prone area, listen out for information on cerealogists' plans, viewing-points, equipment, weapons, etc. They may be planning your demise, and any hindrance of your work-in-progress could be humiliating. Resist the temptation, however, to engage in conversation, as pointless arguments and even violence may ensue.

THE DROP OFF:

Making sure you haven't been followed, drive to your chosen site and unload the roller and stalk-stomper. Leave them in a recognisable place, such as a gate or a large bush, to make them easy to find in the dark. Then park your car in the nearest village – empty cars in isolated places may attract suspicion – and stealthily walk back to the field.

CREATING THE FORMATION:

Remember, criminal damage is an offence. Always be sure to use the tram or tractor lines to get to your starting point. While some circlemakers prefer to engage in preliminary rituals to ensure speed, stamina, genuineness, or to encourage future circles growth, this is not obligatory for the beginner.

Establish the centre of your first circle about two metres in from the tram-line, walking in a curved loping stride so as not to leave an obvious trail – a sure sign of human involvement.

Make the centre by turning on the axis of your standing foot whilst dragging crop down with the other. A beautifully nested centre – more proof of genuineness – can be fashioned by hand. This will also increase the likelihood of positive results in any subsequent micro-biological study.

If you are working alone, place a metal skewer in or near the centre, attaching your tape through the loop before measuring your chosen radius. For large circles or rings over 60 metres in diameter, tapes can be joined or extended with string. Pulling the tape taught to ensure accuracy, walk in the same direction as your centre, leaving a narrow trail through the crop, eventually returning to your starting point. You are now ready to roll, or stomp, the circle.

N.B. Sometimes even a slight breeze is enough to cause the tape to vibrate, making a mysterious whooping noise. Do not be alarmed. This noise has been identified by cerealogists as an effect of the True Circlemakers.

SIGNS OF GENUINENESS

Flow, and multiple layering:
A circle flattened outwards from the centre will produce a radial lay, made famous by the original circlemakers 'Doug and Dave', and especially revered by "the world's foremost authority on crop circles" Colin Andrews. Working inwards from the perimeter will result in a near concentric flow, "like water"

according to expert George Wingfield. Both are regarded as genuine, unhoaxable effects. As is practically anything else; the experts' wide latitude for genuineness permits great freedom of expression. As well as circles, avenues, crescents, key shapes, rings and arcs – any increase in complexity – will prove popular.

Always check you have not left anything behind: string, empty beer cans, sweet wrappers, etc. Rubbish creates work for early-bird researchers who will not want it to be mistaken for evidence of human involvement.

Grapeshot:
Even the experts now concede that 'grapeshot' – small circles outside the main pattern – can be hoaxed. Moreover, compulsively making these circles as you walk out of the field leaves a really naff trail to your exit. Much better to save your energies to make a bigger or more intricate formation.

SURE SIGNS OF GENUINENESS:

You are not caught making it.

It is discovered in convenient proximity to any crop circle research group.

A FORMATION WILL DEVELOP ITS OWN FOLKLORE IF:

1. The pattern is of symbolic importance and is therefore useful on the proselyting lecture circuit – e.g. mandalas, fractals, Atlantean script, etc.

2. It is made in a field which cerealogists claim to have been watching when the formation appeared.

3. Light and/or audio phenomena are associated with it.

4. Mysterious substances of confirmed extraterrestrial origins (not beer cans, sweet wrappers, iron filings, etc) are found in it.

5. A publicised prediction is circulated beforehand. If it is proclaimed more than once by the same individual, paid opportunities (TV interviews, etc) or invitations to lecture may follow. For circlemakers wishing to pursue these opportunities it is crucial to maintain an enigmatic air at all times, and to not talk exclusively of your own formations (a dead give away to any sceptics in the audience).

SCIENTIFIC ANALYSIS:

Doug Bower (right) and Dave Chorley.

In attempting to gain widespread acceptance of crop circles' anomalous nature, cerealogists pretend a curious relationship with conventional science. Phrases such as 'we are working closely with scientists', or 'we are awaiting the results of analysis' are frequently brayed. Similarly, some investigators claim to have discovered a 'litmus test' to quickly determine 'hoaxed' circles from 'genuine', deploying all manner of finely-tuned instruments – electron microscopes, magnetometers, compasses, dowsing rods, resonating bowls, fluttering chakras, black boxes with wires, aerials, dials and probes, etc. – to underscore their expertise. Whilst impressive, such behaviour contradicts their general rejection of scientific principles. More importantly, however, it provides a valuable sense of security to those who cite the need for only one circle to be proved 'of unknown origin' in order to justify pursuing the entire phenomenon – an heroic search for the elusive 'white crow'.

It is just as important for beginners to appreciate that as a 'new science' cerealogy embraces relativism as the route to ultimate truth. Steer clear of explanation, and encourage circular argument. By disowning authorship of your work, the Hypothetical Unseen Hoaxer (HUH) helps researchers to place the burden of proof upon followers of the most reasonable hypothesis, thereby adding weight to the most unreasonable hypotheses. One measures such circularity beginning anywhere. Jump in and enjoy.

Edited by Rob Irving from *'The Beginner's Guide to Circlemaking'*. (1994) by Rob Irving and John Lundberg. For more information see *http://www.circlemakers.org*

WITCH GUIDE

The days of cackling crones riding broomsticks through the night may be long gone, but witches still cast a powerful spell the world over.

www.arttoday.com

MEDIUM WHO GOT THE MESSAGE

A group of campaigners is attempting to have the last conviction under the 1753 Witchcraft Act overturned. Helen Duncan was arrested during a seancé in Portsmouth in 1944, and was charged with "pretending to raise the spirits of the dead". She was given nine months in Holloway Prison, and died in November 1956, following another police raid on a séance. Now, a campaign to have her name cleared has been started by members of the British Society of Paranormal Investigators; her case has also been seized upon by *Psychic News* as a cornerstone of their current campaign to have pardoned all the psychics convicted under the 1753 Act and its successor, the 1955 Fraudulent Mediums Act.

Duncan's case is certainly remarkable. It was widely rumoured that she was regarded as a security risk following a curious incident involving a wartime cover up. In 1941, she held a séance in which the spirit of a dead sailor reportedly appeared and told the assembled spectators "my ship has sunk." His ship was the *HMS Barham*, which had sunk shortly before. However, the Admiralty had hushed up news of the loss of the *Barham* for reasons of morale, and many believe that Duncan's subsequent prosecution and imprisonment represented an attempt

to prevent her from revealing any further potentially damaging information which might come through from the spirit world; our sources suggest that there was a real worry that Duncan might accidentally reveal the site of the D-Day landings.

The head of Military Intelligence in Scotland, Brig. Firebrace, certainly seemed to see it this way; in 1959, he wrote, 'Mrs Duncan was a somewhat

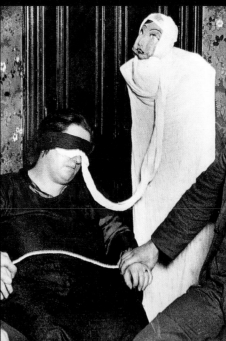

CONVINCING?: Helen Duncan materialises a spirit guide.

dangerous person... Scotland Yard [consulted] as to how Mrs D could be prevented from giving this information out... it was authentic.' Churchill is

known personally to have been outraged at her arrest, more for financial than moral reasons. 'Give me a report of the 1753 Witchcraft Act,' he wrote in a letter to the Home Secretary. 'What was the cost of a trial to the State in which the Recorder was kept busy with all of this obsolete tomfoolery?'

The new campaign to have her pardoned certainly takes the view that she was a victim of a conspiracy to silence her. They are currently appealing for funds and legal assistance to help them review court documents from her trial and formulate a formal appeal to the Home Office. One of those involved, psychic investigator Leslie Price, says that 'it has always been believed that the reason for her arrest was security. The problem is that papers relating to cases such as this remain secret for 75 years, and in that case we are having difficulty getting to the truth.'

There seems to have been little progress in Duncan's case so far. Although the appeal was the subject of a programme in Channel 4's *Secret History* series in July, at the time of writing it still looks unlikely that there will be any significant developments in the near future. The Criminal Cases Review Commission has refused to refer her case to the court of appeal.

MEPL

AFRICAN **WITCHCRAFT**

Some African countries, however, seem to take witchcraft all too seriously. For some years now, *Fortean Times* has had a steady stream of reports regarding the growth of belief in witchcraft in Africa. In many cases, sorcerers are believed to make men's penises vanish simply by shaking hands with them. While this may sound somewhat unlikely, many people have been killed; lynch mobs in Senegal have burned and beaten to death at least eight alleged sorcerers suspected of having this improbable power, with many other people seriously injured. Papers in Dakar published pictures of suspected "genital thieves" killed by angry crowds and *Le Matin* asked in a banner headline: "Have we lost our common sense?" Three of the deaths were in Dakar, while *Le Soleil* reported that five people from Niger had been killed by mobs in Ziguinghor, southern Casamance province.

On the Ivory Coast, a 60-year-old man was hacked to death by a mob of villagers who accused him of killing a young boy by witchcraft. The daily paper *Le Jour* reported that two other people in the village of Godilehiry, in the south of the country, had been lynched over the boy's death. The parents of 11-year-old Christophe Adou, who had died under unusual circumstances, consulted their son's corpse to discover the identity of the murderer.

Slightly less gruesome, and significantly more odd, is the case of the flying wizards currently afflicting Zambia – at least, according to reports in the *Times* of Zambia. In April, the family of the late Angus Ngulube had gathered for his funeral; after night fell, his widow, Joyce Mbewe, and other members of the extended family were sleeping when a gale began to blow outside. They heard a heavy object hit the roof, roll off and hit the ground. A male voice, speaking in Bemba, asked to be allowed in, crying, "Mother of Banda, open up. How can you leave me outside, I want to come inside."

After some time, Ngulube's stepson William took a look outside, but could see nothing out of the ordinary. Soon after, his aunt, Asineli Soko, found an object by the

door which the *Times* describes as "a small humanoid creature whose features varied from a cat to an owl". The creature had lion-like claws, and something referred to as "shiny red and white beads which changed to yellow and red at daybreak". One of its feet was injured, and its blood had begun to stain the ground. Gradually, as they watched, it began to assume human shape.

Mbewe called for her neighbours and family, who surrounded the creature and began to question it. She reports that "He claimed to have come from Mununga on an aeroplane and that he had come to eat meat from his grandfather. My stepson asked him whether he knew him, and he agreed, saying he looked like Dag Hammerskjöld." [The UN Secretary-General who died in a plane crash in Ndola in 1961]

The "wizard" was taken to police, where he claimed to be Kalasa Nswiba of Nswiba village. He claimed that he had been flying over the area in a magical aircraft, but had crashed when flying over Ngulube's house because his family had fortified the place with "strong juju". The aircraft, he said, had been travelling from Kasam to Mporokos, with six other passengers. Police said he was to be charged with witchcraft.

The Zambian government took a keen interest in the case, with the Permanent Secretary to Northern Province Minister Daniel Kapapa officially ordered to assist with the investigations. Kapapa said that the government was keen to find out "whether the suspect really existed" and whether he had been in the area the day before he turned out at the Ngulube household. Meanwhile, the Traditional Health Practitioners Association of Zambia issued a statement saying that the suspect's story sounded as if it could be true, and called upon the government to legalise witch-hunting.

Later reports from the *Times* of Zambia suggest that some people aren't waiting for it to be legalised. One, a Congolese known only as Matanda, has been roaming the Samfya area, seizing villagers' property and arresting them for witchcraft. Matanda can be seen

each morning flogging his captives and forcing them to drink unidentified concoctions as part of their "cleansing rites". As with the witch mania in Britain and America, villagers were reported to be in terror; one, who did not want to be named, complained on national radio that villagers were starving because they were afraid to go out to work the fields. The witchfinder's motives seem reasonably transparent; a common complaint is that property such as bicycles, sewing machines and livestock is often siezed as a "fine" for witchcraft.

DEAD GORGEOUS

A MASS panic about a supposed plague of zombies created by witches has gripped central Java, although opinions are divided as to what the creatures – known locally as *hanto pocong* – actually look like; some say they are goat-like creatures, others that they are beautiful women, while still others that they are tall, pale people who give off a nasty smell. One woman who thought she had seen a zombie called for a neighbour, who fiercely attacked it with a machete. It turned out to be a banana tree.

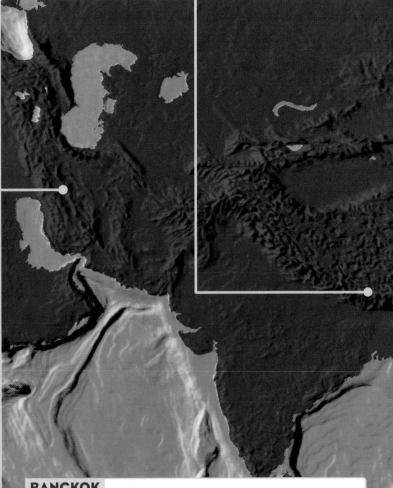

IRAN

Mohammad Ali Maasoomi, 67, a farmer from Bojnoord in Iran, doesn't feel extremes of heat and cold. He sleeps naked in snow every day for two hours. He answered the door to the journalist from the *Hamshahri* newspaper in summer clothes, even though it was 19 F (-7 C). He travelled to Mecca last year and thought nothing of walking and praying in the blazing sun of 122 F (50 C). Mr Maasoomi noticed his strange immunity when he was 10. "I can adjust my body temperature," he said. "I inherited the ability from my father and now my son has inherited it from me."

IRAN

Seid Ali Saedi, a university student in Tebriz, bought 200 goldfish in March 1993. He experimented with their diet, feeding them protein, vitamin C, parsley extract and other things. One fish was particularly tolerant of a varied diet and seemed more alert than the others. Sometimes he put a loudspeaker next to the aquarium and played music to the fish; there was no reaction except with the special fish, which moved back and forth nervously until the music was turned down. "By December 1996," said Mr Saedi, "only 12 fish had survived. I kept them in a pond in my yard. That winter the water froze to a depth of one centimetre (0.4in). The ice broke and all the fish died, except the special one. It was crawling around the ice, putting snowflakes in its mouth." On 12 May 1997, he went to change the pond water and noticed a floating object. On further examination he found that a grain of wheat had stuck in the fish's gullet and had begun to sprout. It had three small blades, up to 11cm (4in) long. Mr Saedi had thrown wheat grains in the pond as fish food. Astonishingly, the fish survived another month. Mr Neishabouri, professor of biology at Tebriz University, examined the fish. "The grain had stuck in the inner part of the fish's gill and sprouted, growing in darkness. The sprout spread its roots into the gills, stifling the fish so that it couldn't open its mouth." Mr Saedi put the fish/plant in formalin and then in cold water. The sprout then continued to grow.

IRAN

Throughout 13 years of marriage, Fariboorz hoped to have a son and blamed his wife for bearing a daughter. She became pregnant again. During her labour in hospital, Fariboorz threatened her, saying: "If you don't bear a son, I will cut your daughter's hands." The nurses hustled him out and in an hour the baby was born. "Is it a boy or a girl?" Fariboorz asked a nurse anxiously. The reply: "It's a boy sir, but... he has got a deformed hand." Fariboorz began crying and recalled his cruel threat.

KATHMANDU

Kalyana Thapa, 27, a widow and mother of three, was told in a dream where to dig for idols. Soon afterwards, she pinpointed the exact spot by pitching her trishai (trident) on a rubbish mound at Lalitpur sub-metropolis ward no. 13, Kusunti, in Kathmandu. She seemed "possessed", shaking, jumping, running and urging the locals to help her dig out the hidden idols.

At first, "unruly persons" tried to "manhandle" the widow; but eventually a couple of locals excavated the mound, and found a shiva lingam (stone phallus representing the god Shiva) and three idols of sitting bulls. One report said live snakes were also found. Radhesyam Dhungana, an elderly local resident, said that people long ago used to pour water over a bull idol which used to be slightly visible on the surface. However, it was a mystery how an illiterate widow knew where to dig, as she was not local but came from Kavre district.

Within weeks, thousands of people from all over Kathmandu were queuing daily to pay homage to the idols and have a darshan (audience) with the widow, who has been locally honoured with the title of Mataji (honoured mother). On one day alone, between 25,000 and 30,000 people came to the site, according to Mrs Madhavi Subba, chair of the 51-member committee formed to build a two-storey temple on the site, to be called Pancheshwar Temple.

BANGKOK

The skulls and bones of 21,347 people were stacked in a grisly display in preparation for what is believed to have been the largest religious cremation ceremony ever performed. The remains, all unidentified or unclaimed, were moved in November from a pauper's cemetery in Bangkok run by Po Teck Tung, a Chinese benevolent association, to make way for a motorway. There were five days of funerary rites with dozens of people sprinkling the bones with fragrant water or laying gold leaf on skulls in preparation for the cremation. People believe they gain religious merit from such ceremonies.

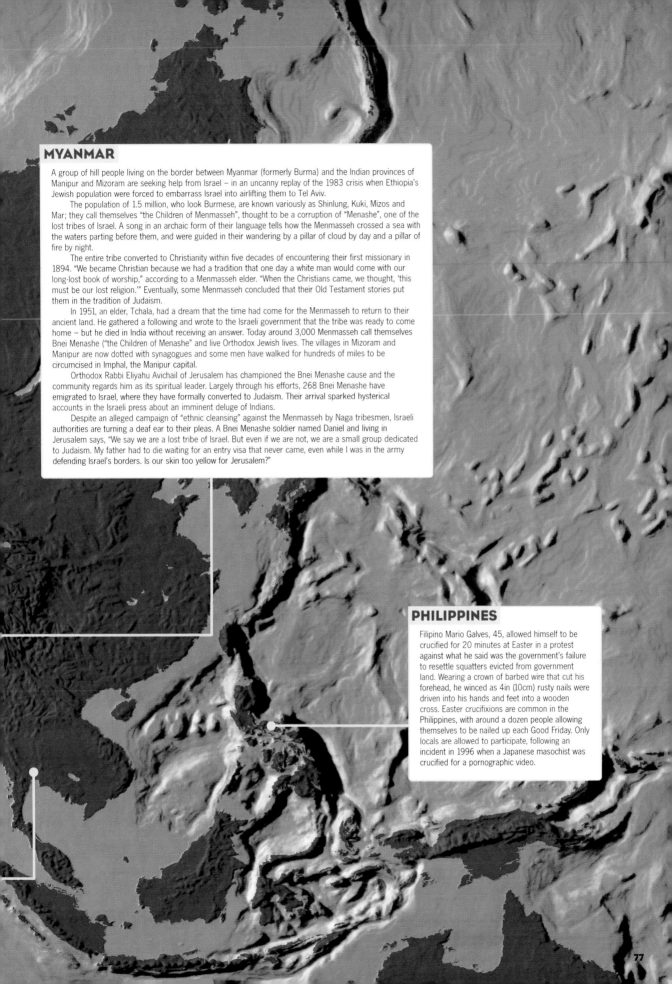

MYANMAR

A group of hill people living on the border between Myanmar (formerly Burma) and the Indian provinces of Manipur and Mizoram are seeking help from Israel – in an uncanny replay of the 1983 crisis when Ethiopia's Jewish population were forced to embarrass Israel into airlifting them to Tel Aviv.

The population of 1.5 million, who look Burmese, are known variously as Shinlung, Kuki, Mizos and Mar; they call themselves "the Children of Menmasseh", thought to be a corruption of "Menashe", one of the lost tribes of Israel. A song in an archaic form of their language tells how the Menmasseh crossed a sea with the waters parting before them, and were guided in their wandering by a pillar of cloud by day and a pillar of fire by night.

The entire tribe converted to Christianity within five decades of encountering their first missionary in 1894. "We became Christian because we had a tradition that one day a white man would come with our long-lost book of worship," according to a Menmasseh elder. "When the Christians came, we thought, 'this must be our lost religion.'" Eventually, some Menmasseh concluded that their Old Testament stories put them in the tradition of Judaism.

In 1951, an elder, Tchala, had a dream that the time had come for the Menmasseh to return to their ancient land. He gathered a following and wrote to the Israeli government that the tribe was ready to come home – but he died in India without receiving an answer. Today around 3,000 Menmasseh call themselves Bnei Menashe ("the Children of Menashe" and live Orthodox Jewish lives. The villages in Mizoram and Manipur are now dotted with synagogues and some men have walked for hundreds of miles to be circumcised in Imphal, the Manipur capital.

Orthodox Rabbi Eliyahu Avichail of Jerusalem has championed the Bnei Menashe cause and the community regards him as its spiritual leader. Largely through his efforts, 268 Bnei Menashe have emigrated to Israel, where they have formally converted to Judaism. Their arrival sparked hysterical accounts in the Israeli press about an imminent deluge of Indians.

Despite an alleged campaign of "ethnic cleansing" against the Menmasseh by Naga tribesmen, Israeli authorities are turning a deaf ear to their pleas. A Bnei Menashe soldier named Daniel and living in Jerusalem says, "We say we are a lost tribe of Israel. But even if we are not, we are a small group dedicated to Judaism. My father had to die waiting for an entry visa that never came, even while I was in the army defending Israel's borders. Is our skin too yellow for Jerusalem?"

PHILIPPINES

Filipino Mario Galves, 45, allowed himself to be crucified for 20 minutes at Easter in a protest against what he said was the government's failure to resettle squatters evicted from government land. Wearing a crown of barbed wire that cut his forehead, he winced as 4in (10cm) rusty nails were driven into his hands and feet into a wooden cross. Easter crucifixions are common in the Philippines, with around a dozen people allowing themselves to be nailed up each Good Friday. Only locals are allowed to participate, following an incident in 1996 when a Japanese masochist was crucified for a pornographic video.

Top 10 Natural Stories

1 ALIEN SEAWEED

MARINE RESEARCHERS in Stuttgart accidentally created a "monster" seaweed during experiments in the 1970s, and the mutant is now reportedly threatening the entire Mediterranean ecosystem. The weed, created by exposing a Pacific seaweed to ultraviolet light and selectively breeding it, is thought to have accidentally been flushed into the sea when the Wilhelmina Zoo flushed out their tanks in the mid-80s. It now covers 8,000 acres (3,200 hectares) of the seabed, and is destroying sea-grass beds where many species spawn. It is also feared to be toxic to indigenous fish. Snails which live on the seaweed have been specially bred in a laboratory in Nice, but French officials are reluctant to release them for fear of causing yet another environmental catastrophe.

3 FATAL METEORITE

THE FIRST recorded meteorite fatality occured in Colombia as fireballs were seen shooting across the sky over most of the country. Four children died in Bogota when their home burned down; a hole 10in (24cm) across was found in the tin roof of their shack, edged with traces of sulphur. The local fire chief suggested the meteorite explanation after all other causes were ruled out; the shack had no electricity, and the fire was not started by a candle or gas lamp. He said he had seen fireballs in the sky when he arrived at the scene.

2 LETHAL JELLY

JONATHAN BALDWIN

RESIDENTS OF the Hungarian town of Dombegyhaz are in fear of their lives after a mysterious "amoeba-like" substance was sprayed over the town by three glowing yellow spheres. The substance, which a Budapest researcher said was "not unlike a mucus tropical fungus", is being blamed for a series of strange illnesses, unexplained deaths and animal birth defects. Several animals have since been born with extra or missing limbs and strange cauliflower-like growths. The owners of all the animals subsequently died from virulent cancerous growths.

4 BUBBLING RIVERS OF FLAME

THE CATARACT river in New South Wales has become so polluted that if you throw a match into it near Woollongong, the water is liable to burst into flames 20in (50cm) high. Locals are worried about the risk of bush fires and injuries to children. A national research organisation has blamed a mixture of methane, carbon dioxide and trace amounts of other gasses which is seeping from a coal mine beneath the river.

JONATHAN BALDWIN

www.arttoday.com

⑤ BOLT FROM THE BLUE

CHRISTIAN PILGRIMS cried "It's a miracle!" and "Jesus is coming!" when lightning struck the dome of the 12th centruy Mosque of Omar next to the Church of the Holy Sephulcre in Jerusalem. The strike took place during an Orthodox foot-washing ceremony in the run-up to Easter; the ceremony's site is popularly believed to be where the Resurrection took place. Pilgrims were showered with stones blown from the mosque.

⑥ HARD CELL

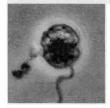

A PREVIOUSLY harmless microbe has mutated into a fish killer. *Pfiesteria piscicida* was discovered in South Carolina when it began to kill fish by stunning them before literally eating them alive. In an experiment, *Pfiesteria* was introduced to a human blood sample; it immediately devoured all the blood cells. Research has shown that the microbes are almost indestructable, capable of surviving at least half an hour in sulphuric acid. They are now thought to be colonising the North Sea, having crossed the Atlantic in the bilges and ballast tanks of American cargo ships.

⑦ STUMPED AGAIN

THE STUMPS of some 200 sitka, spruce and cedar trees have been uncovered after two thousand years thanks to the actions of the infamous El Niño weather system. Crashing waves from Niño storms on the coast of Oregon near Neskowin exposed the gnarled stumps in March, and they soon became a tourist attraction. Sadly, they have gradually been reclaimed by the beach as sands were redepositied by natural wave action.

AP/THE OREGONIAN

⑧ ICE STORM

CANADA WAS devastated by ice storms which caused an estimated $2 billion in damage. At the height of the storms, three million Canadians were left without power when pylons collapsed under the weight of accumulated ice. Almost every aspect of life was disrupted, with parts of Quebec and Montreal declared danger zones because of the danger of falling ice. Taking wind chill into account, temperatures dropped to -20°C, and at least 20 people died from hypothermia or carbon monoxide poisoning caused by using barbecues as emergency heating. The production of Canada's famous maple syrup was threatened after an estimated 20 million maple trees were split in half by the weight of ice on their branches.

⑨ CLOUDS OF ILL OMEN

HERBERT DÖHRING, the former major domo of Hitler's retreat at Berghof has spoken for the first time about his time with the former German dictator, and described a bizarre occurrence just before the outbreak of war. In August 1939, as von Ribbentrop met with Stalin in Moscow, Hitler and his entourage gathered on the Berghof balcony. Tensions were high, when Hitler recieved a call saying Stalin was demanding control of the Baltic states. Döhring recalled that the sky suddenly went into turmoil: "It was blood red, green, sulphur grey, black as the night, a jagged yellow." One of Hitler's entourage warned Hitler that "This means blood, blood, and more blood, destruction and suffering." Many historians believe that losing Stalin's co-operation ultimately cost Hitler the war.

⑩ GIANT PUFFBALL

MAUREEN JACKSON (right) discovered a 20in (50cm)-wide puffball mushroom (*Calvatia gigantes*) at her parent's farm in Roxby, near Staithes, North Yorkshire. It weighed 16lb 4oz (7.4kg). An even bigger puffball was found two months later in Todmorden, West Yorkshire, by Stephen and Olwen Helliwell. This one weighed 21lb (9.5kg) and was 64in (163cm) in circumference.

TERRY REED

SCIENCE**FRONTIERS**

The year's most intriguing science
stories from around the world, gathered
by WILLIAM CORLISS.

BIOLOGY

LUNACY IN TREES

MORE THAN half a century ago, biologist H.S. Burr inserted electrodes into trees and found that the voltages between them varied with the phase of the Moon. It has now been discovered that the diameters of tree stems also bloat and shrink with the position of the Moon in the sky. There is a tide in the affairs of trees, it seems. If tides occur twice a day, so do the swellings and shrinkings of trees. These tidal patterns are evident even when the trees are kept in darkness and at constant pressure and humidity. Even more surprising, chunks of tree stems that are sealed to prevent water from flowing in or out will still expand and contract according to the 24-hour,49-minute lunar cycle as long as the cambium, the most active growing region, survives. The dimensional changes are small – only tenths of a millimetre, but even these seem too large, given the weakness of the moon's gravitational field here on earth.

TELESTOMPING ELEPHANTS

ELEPHANTS, RHINOS, okapis and even some birds use infrasound (frequencies below 20 Hertz) for communication. University of California researchers recently reported that elephants also send low-frequency acoustic signals by stomping the ground. Almost inaudible in the air, the sounds travel through the ground and can be picked up by ground microphones. It's thought that this communication channel has a range of as much as 56 kilometres (37.3 miles) – far greater than the sounds could be perceived in the air. Supporting this notion, anecdotes say that elephants somehow know when other elephants are being killed far, far away. They run in the opposite direction! But how do they detect the stomping sounds if they travel through the ground?

IMMENSE SPERM ARE NUTRITIOUS TOO

FRUIT FLIES smaller than a tomato seed produce sperm almost 6 cm (2.3 inches) long. These can be seen coiled up in the tiny fertilised eggs. Why so long? Perhaps they carry nourishment for the developing embryo.

TOMATOES SEE RED. AND OTHER COLOURS TOO

PLANT LEAVES, it turns out, contain light-sensitive pigments similar to those in the human retina. The plants do not "see", but the pigments provide environmental information. Plant leaves reflect infrared light well, so when a tomato plant's pigments detect a lot of infrared, the plant "thinks" that it may be crowded out by competing vegetation. The tomato plant responds aggressively by growing more rapidly.

GARDENING TIP: Red plastic mulch placed between rows of tomato plants reflects a lot of infrared light, so tricking them into accelerating their growth.

HUMANS ON THE MENU FOR SPIDERS AND SNAILS?

ONE OF the world's most poisonous creatures, the Australian funnel web spider, has a poison deadly only to insects and humans – all other mammals are apparently immune. Of 45 component parts in the poison, one specifically attacks insect brain cells, the other human ones. Similarly the venom of the cone shell snail is lethal to humans. But why? We're hardly likely to be considered practical prey by either of these critters.

ARCHÆOLOGY

THOSE ANCIENT GREEK PYRAMIDS

ON GREEK soil, at Hellenikon and Ligourio, west of Athens in the Argolid region, are two limestone pyramids very much like those at Giza near Cairo. The big difference is size; the Greek pyramids are only the size of a large room compared to the Great Pyramid's height (with capstone) of almost 500ft (151m). The dating of crystals from internal surfaces of the limestone blocks dates the Hellenikon pyramid to 2730 BC and the Ligourie, to 2260 BC. So the Greek pyramids were built in roughly the same time frame as the Egyptian pyramids. The classical scholar Pausanias wrote in the 2nd century AD. that the Hellenikon pyramid was a cenotaph for the deed fallen in a fratricidal battle 4,000 years ago. Nobody believed his story until now.

WOODHENGES BEFORE PYRAMIDS

THE SOIL signatures of a 5,000-year-old wooden structure were discovered at Stanton Drew, in South-Western England last year near the Great Circle of standing stones.
There were once 400-500 oak pillars on the site, probably a metre (3.3ft) in diameter, 8 metres (26ft) high, and weighing 5 tons each. The nine concentric rings of pillars occupied an area about 100 metres in diameter. Although probably too large to have been roofed, the oak columns might have been carved or decorated. The questions, as always, is why?

GEOLOGY

THE BIG CRACK

THE DEVASTATING effect of tidal waves was demonstrated in Papua New Guinea this year. Recent discoveries in Hawaii suggest that Australia, Japan and California should also prepare for a seaside assault. There is geological evidence in New South Wales, Australia, that part of the coast was scoured by a tsunami generated in Hawaii 100,000 years ago. The postulated wave started about 375m (1237.5ft) high in Hawaii and was 40m (132ft) by the time it reached Australia. Currently a 4,760 cubic mile chunk of Hawaii, known as the Hilina Slump, is breaking away at the rate of 4 inches (10m) per year. It's said to be the fastest moving tract of land on earth for its size. In November 1975, a 37 mile (60km) wide section dropped 11.5ft (34.8m), sliding 25ft (7.6m) towards the sea. If the whole block broke off at once, it could create a tsunami 1,000ft (303m) high.

PSYCHOLOGY

TACTILE VENTRILOQUISM

IS THE name given to an eerie psychological experiment invented at the University of Pittsburgh. Why not try it on your friends?
Step 1: The subject rests his or her arm and hand on a table but is prevented from seeing them by a screen.
Step 2: A realistic rubber arm and hand are placed next to the real arm and hand but on the other side of the screen, and in full view of the subject.
Step 3: The experimenter strokes each hand simultaneously with small paintbrushes.
Result: The subject thinks that the rubber band is his or her own and belongs to his or her body.
Step 4: The experimenter strokes only the rubber hand.
Result: The subject claims his or her hand has become numb.

ASTRONOMY

THE "STEALTH" REGION OF MARS

FOR SOME 2,060 km (1,373 miles) along the Martian equator west of Arsia Mons and Pavonis Mons stretches an area that is invisible to terrestrial radar. Of course, we can see this region but, when a 3cm (1in) radar is pointed at it, no detectable echoes are returned. Thus the term "stealth," as in the F-117 Stealth aircraft. Are the clever Martians trying to conceal something from prying Earthlings? Unfortunately not. Loose, unconsolidated sediments are poor reflectors of radar waves. Examinations of Viking-Orbiter photos tell geologists that the "stealth" region is almost certainly thickly strewn with volcanic ash, which would absorb the radar waves very well.

SCIENCE FRONTIERS, edited by Wiliam Corliss, is a bimonthly collection of digests of scientific anomalies from the current literature. Published by the **Sourcebook Project, P.O. Box 107, Glen Arm, MD 21057**. Annual subscription: $7.00.

WOODHENGE: Ancient millennium dome?

THE **RISE** AND **FALL** OF THE MARTIAN EMPIRE

New photographs have finally brought an end to speculation about the "Face" on Mars. Or have they? Theodolyte in hand, MARK PILKINGTON surveys the damage.

O ur nearest planetary neighbour has been a source of constant fascination for human kind. As god of war and agriculture, and father of Romulus and Remus, Mars was second only to Jupiter in the ancient Roman pantheon. To astrologers it was "the little troublemaker" – a name that has proved uncannily appropriate in describing its relationship with scientists and dreamers of every age.

Last April, years of intense speculation, heightened by the now-disputed 1996 discovery of martian microbes on a meteorite, were abruptly ended. Bowing to public pressure, NASA sent the Mars Global Surveyor (MGS) over the Cydonia region to photograph what for many was the final proof of an extraterrestrial civilisation – the mile-long "face". The MGS's equipment would produce images around 10 times clearer than those delivered by the original Viking Probe in 1976. The world held its breath. Multiple mirrors of the NASA/Jet Propulsion Labs web site strained under the load as millions of eager visitors waited for their first glimpse of what may have been both our ancient past and our far future.

But alas, the face was nothing but cosmic debris, a Rorschach blot of epic proportions. This was not the first post-Viking attempt to re-examine the enigmatic region. In fact all three previous efforts, by two Russian probes in 1989 and NASA's $1.5 billion Mars Observer in August 1993, had ended with the mysterious disappearances of the craft. NASA's Observer lost contact just three days before it was due to enter Mars orbit. Not surprisingly, many smelled a rat, the cover-up of a cosmic calling card – the ultimate evidence of an alien intel-

tecting themselves from their troublesome neighbours or an earthbound secret government, protecting us from a truth too awesome to contemplate?

First spotted in 1976, the face was dismissed by NASA scientists as a trick of light and shadow. It wasn't until the early 90s that it returned to public prominence through the tireless PR work of Richard Hoagland and his group, "The Enterprise Mission". Hoagland, a one-time NASA consultant, lectured tirelessly about the cosmic meaning implicit in not only the Mars face, but the whole Cydonia region. Sure enough, the harder he looked at his heavily-computer-enhanced Viking images, the more he found what he was looking for. Eventually he had discovered a whole range of geographical anomalies in the area, including a half-mile-high tetrahedral pyramid, a city, a wall, a huge mound (The Tholus) and a crater or reservoir. Drawing complex geometrical parallels between Cydonia and Egypt's Giza plateau, Hoagland felt that he had proved a correspondence between Mars' face, the Sphinx and the pyramids at both locations. Mirrored onto itself the Martian face took on a leonine appearance, making it part man, part lion – like the Sphinx. Others thought it resembled Swamp Thing or a Cyberman from *Dr Who*. But it didn't stop there.

A Rorschach blot of epic proportions

English photographer David Percy joined more dots to show that a carefully scaled map of the Cydonia region, if superimposed over an Ordinance Survey map of Avebury in Wiltshire, produced further remarkable correspondences. If the enigmatic Silbury Hill was mapped onto the

CYDONIA: facing the facts

Tholus, then Avebury's Neolithic stone circle fitted over Cydonia's crater with uncanny precision. For Hoagland and others this, along with the data from Giza and also Mexico's Avenue of the Dead, proved that whoever built the Martian complex must also have been involved in the devlopment of early human civilisation on Earth. For Percy, however, things got considerably more complex. Combining telepathically-received messages from higher plabes with the Cydonian data and information gleaned from studying crop circle patterns, he showed that both the Avebury ring and Cydonia crater had

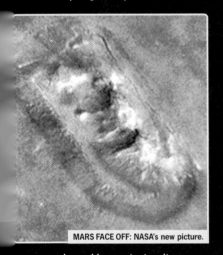

MARS FACE OFF: NASA's new picture.

once housed huge spinning discs. These were advanced hyperdimensional power sources that, with only the energy input of two meditating people wearing pointy hats, could generate enough power for a whole continent. Hoping perhaps that the discs would generate funds for a prototype like they did energy – at least in his own mind – Percy outlined his ideas in fictional form in the very large and staggeringly odd book, *Two Thirds*. A prototype disc has yet to appear.

Other authors drew equally grand conclusions, though with greater financial and critical success. Most notable was Graham Hancock, whose book on the mysterious origins of the Sphinx, *Fingerprints of the Gods*, was a huge bestseller. Though Hancock only hinted at the Cydonia connection, it was certainly there, and also had something to do with Atlantis.

ject was excised from the book by concerned publishers. This chapter reappeared in expanded form in 1998 with what might be deemed inauspicious timing. Hancock, along with Graham Bauval and John Grigsby, released their book *The Mars Mystery* within weeks of the Surveyor images' unveiling . The face, they tell us, is a warning from the past about our possibly cataclysmic future. Readers voted with their wallets, apparently taking the authors' word over NASA's. *The Mars Mystery*'s message was similar to that proclaimed by author and alien confidant Whitley Strieber in his 1997 book, *The Secret School*. Strieber described the red planet's lifelong importance to him and, by consequence, its importance to the rest of mankind – again, a warning about the future. He claimed that childhood visions had seen him exploring the Martian face and pyramids decades before the first Viking images were beamed to Earth. Strangely, he'd never seen fit to mention them in any of his other three alien contact books.

But Richard Hoagland, Graham Hancock and colleagues were by no means the first to lose face over the red planet. In 1877, Italian astronomer Giovanni Schiaparelli announced his discovery of what appeared to be straight lines etched onto the surface of the planet. He called them "canali", meaning channels. The news was swiftly picked up by the English-speaking world, who saw these "canals" as a sign that Mars did indeed harbour intelligent life. Chief amongst the idea's proponents was distinguished American astronomer Percival Lowell, who was the first to suggest

He immediately denounced them as "useless"

the existence of the planet Pluto, at the time invisible to the naked eye. Lowell wrote three books about Mars – *Mars and its Canals*, *Mars as the Abode of Life* and *The Evolution of Worlds* – which he regarded as a planet at the end of its natural inhabitable life span. Once green and pleasant it was now an arid, dusty wilderness; the canals the last hallmarks of an ancient

Martian trailer trash?

and advanced civilisation. Such ideas were extremely influential, most famously inspiring HG Wells' *War of the Worlds*. Today Schiaparelli's "canali" are known to have been an optical illusion – dots on the planet's surface connected to form straight lines by people peering through old-fashioned telescopes. Sound familiar?

Reactions to the latest Mars Global Surveyor pictures have been predictably extreme. Hoagland immediately denounced them as "useless" and "crap", claiming that they were taken at only two thirds (that fraction again) the equipment's capability. Scientists in the original pro-face camp were more reasonable. Photoanalyst Dr Mark Carlotto, one of the very first to take an interest in Cydonia, conceded that the object now seemed "less remarkable", though he still insists that parts of the mound appear to be unusually flattened and bevelled. Along with Professor Stanley McDaniel, whose 1993 report was influential in NASA's decision to rephotograph the region, Carlotto restated his belief that the now ex-face was only one of a number of Martian anomalies, including "The Cliff", "The String of Beads" (formerly "The Runway") and the "Crater Pyramid". Some hysterical reports accused NASA of having nuked the face to remove the evidence before rephotographing it, others wondered if it might not have fallen down in the last 20 years. Meanwhile, hopeful analysts turned their attentions elsewhere, most spectacularly onto an area dubbed "The Trailer Park", in Mars' southern polar region. Here some see a walled industrial complex and neatly laid out rows of greenhouses.

And what do they grow there? Hopefully NASA's Mars Polar Lander will clear that one up when it visits the

DEEP
ARMAGEDDON!

Meteors are big news, not least because of Hollywood blockbusters like *Deep Impact* and *Armageddon*. Sadly, the truth behind the hundreds of meteor impacts each year is slightly less spectacular – though no less alarming.

www.art

ABSOLUTE BOULDERDASH!

DAVID LEE (below), a retired insurance manager; heard a deafening crash on the roof of his semi-detached house in Hove, Sussex, around midnight on 3 May 1998. A 41b (18kg) lump of rock had shattered roof tiles and bounced onto his garden path. It was black and looked like tarmac, except that it was much harder. "I can only assume it's a meteorite," said Mr Lee, 57. "I don't think anyone could have thrown something that heavy on to the top of the house and caused the tiles to break. It has left quite an indentation." Alternatively, it could be man-made space junk.

SKYWATCHERS THROUGHOUT Britain were treated to a remarkable display of "sky-writing" by a suspected meteor shower in early July. Reports flooded in – mainly from western areas of the country – of vast letters and numbers appearing in the skies. Although meteors were originally ruled out as an explanation, a civilian pilot is reported to have seen a fireball bursting into tiny shards whose smoke trails formed "letters".

TWO LARGE blocks of ice which crashed into the Brazilian state of San Paulo from clear skies are believed to be part of a meteor. The first chunk weighed mere than 110lb (50kg) and tore through the tiled roof of a bus factory in Campinas on 11 July. The second came dawn on 15 July, about 37 miles (60km) north of Campinas, making a small crater. Officials at the local airport ruled out the more conventional explanation of ice from an aircraft, as none was passing at the corresponding times.

JOHN CONNOR PRESS ASSOCIATES (BRIGHTON)

HEAVENLY BOMBARDMENTS

JONATHAN BALDWIN

A 53lb (24kg) boulder fell from the sky into a garden in the Kostroma region, about 200 miles (320km) northeast of Moscow. Konstantin Nechayes, a resident of Ikonnikova village, says the impact created a 3ft (1m) deep crater as it crashed into the ground with a "whip and grinding sound similar to that of a bullet fired from a hunting rifle." He dug out the skull-shaped stone to find it cool to the touch and split in two, revealing an apple-size cavity at its core. Government officials measured the radiation level of the rock, but found nothing unusual. The probable meteorite was sent to the Ministry of the Interior to be analysed.

Something hit southern Greenland – or exploded above it – at the start of the year. Reports from fishermen on three Danish and Norwegian trawlers at widely separated sites on both sides of southern Greenland, say that a flash lasting from two to five seconds lit up the dark sky at 5.11am local time on 9 December. Their sightings were corroborated by video taken by a surveillance camera in a car park in capital, Nuuk. The video, shown repeatedly on Danish television, shows a bright flash of light from a moving source reflected in the curved bonnet of a car. Bjorn Ericksson, first mate on the trawler Regina, saw "a very strong light rolling down from the air. It was like a circle burning, a very strong light blue, and the air around the circle was very light green. The light disappeared in the mountains. It is something from space."

Seismographs in Denmark, Norway, Finland and Germany recorded a 10-second shock, and there are reports of a huge cloud of steam rising from the ice cap after the object descended. The presumptive impact was at 61° 25' N, 44° 26' W, a remote and forbidding site about 30 miles (48km) north-east of Narsursuaq Airport, near the settlement of Qaqortoq (formerly Julianehab).

From descriptions of the steam cloud's size, it has been suggested that as many as five billion tons of ice were vaporised, requiring a substantial meteorite or comet, the mass of which cannot be estimated at present. "According to the accounts, the flash was so huge that we have good reason to believe that this is a giant," said Björn Franck Joegensen of the Tycho Brahe Planetarium in Copenhagen. He said the Qaqortoq meteorite – named, by tradition, after the nearest post office – was likely to have been a one-piece, solid object. It appears to have been travelling at Mach 10 – 7,600mph.

If any solid material remained after the object landed, it might have been hot enough to melt its way through the ice-cap, which would then freeze behind it. The Niels Bohr Institute in Copenhagen estimated that it was probably comparable to the Kap York meteorite that fell south of Thule, Greenland, in prehistoric times. Iron meteorites totalling 50 tons have been collected at the site. Professor Mark Bailey, director of the Armagh Observatory, speculated that the fireball might be linked to the Geminid meteor shower, which occurs annually at this time of year as the Earth passes through the trail of the asteroid Phaeton. A falling spacecraft or other artificial debris re-entering the atmosphere was ruled out.

Research teams were eager to search the area for fragments, but by 22 December, up to 40in (100cm) of snow had fallen in the area and another 10ft (3m) were anticipated before the spring thaw. Attempts to inspect the site from the air were hampered by clouds. The search for a meteorite buried in the Greenland icecap forms the plot of Peter Høeg's best-seller *Miss Smilla's Feeling for Snow.*

SIMULACRA
SPECTACULAR

Photographs of trolls, white elephants, and monsters lurking just beyond the corner of the eye. Captured by the readers of *Fortean Times*.

▲ DAVID SHURVILLE took this photograph in Chiang-Mai, Thailand, in 1994 – he only noticed the cloud resembling a white elephant when the film was developed. It was directly above a golden *chedi* (spire), around the base of which were a number of life-size stone elephants. Directly before the birth of Gautama Buddha, according to legend, his mother dreamed of a white elephant. Consequently in Thailand, albino elephants are revered. Any captured or bred are considered royal property and have to be handed over to the king's stable.

▲ THIS TROLL'S head was captured on film by Jenny Peers next to Skogafoss, a waterfall in southern Iceland, in June 1997.

HONEY BEAR, the kitten on the left, photographed with Tony Unstead of Maidenhead, Berkshire, in 1996, appears to have Rasputin in his ear.

MUFFY THE cat above photographed by Kim Vinall, seems to have a phantom kitten nestling beside her. Some time earlier she had given birth to three kittens, but they were very wild and no home could be found for them. The RSPCA took them away. Perhaps the spirit of one continues to live with Muffy.

TWO WOMEN of the trees. The voluptuous wooden butt was captured in colour by Ray Butler in Beit Road, Lusaka, Zambia; the topless beauty is in Sutton Park, Birmingham, and was pictured by Declan J McCallion.

THIS ROCK face was photographed at Trwyn Maen Melyn on the Lleyn Peninsula near Aberdaron in North Wales by Marjorie Woodcock. Limpets make rather good "teeth", don't they?

THIS CROCODILIAN beastie was photographed at Portgordon on the Moray Firth in Scotland by Kevin McGlue.

THE **FLIGHT** OF THEIR **LIVES**

O N 23 February, from six to 10 El Niño-fuelled tornadoes cut a swathe across Florida from Tampa to Daytona Beach, killing 38 people and injuring more than 250.

JONATHAN WALDICK, an 18-month-old toddler, was in his parents' wood-framed house in Kissimmee when one of the twisters struck, destroying the building. Jonathan and his mattress were carried outside. The 260mph (418kph) wind snapped the top off a large oak tree, then deposited the mattress in the branches. Jonathan landed on top of it as hail and rain pelted the ground and the concrete house next door crumbled. Shirley Driver, the children's great-grandmother, was sleeping in her bed with Jonathan's four-year-old sister, Destiny, when the storm hit. She awoke to find Destiny safe, but Jonathan nowhere in sight. Rescuer Ron Verleson said he feared the worst after searching in vain for 45 minutes after the tornado. It seemed likely that the child was buried under the rubble of his bedroom. "Then we saw his little foot dangling," said Verleson. At first it was thought the toddler was dead, as he lay unmoving and open-eyed. Then his foot moved. "I kept calling his name and he started to whimper," said Verleson. Jonathan's only injury was a small bump on the head.

GARY SEGRAVES, 51, had gone to Laguna Beach, Florida, to rescue his daughter, who had been stranded in a mudslide during the tornadoes. Some strangers offered him a bed for the night, but another mudslide knocked him from the house. When he stopped rolling, he landed on a pile of rocks, twigs and living room furniture next to a cat shelter. Though he had lost his glasses, he noticed that next to him was a baby; "I pinched its fingers to see if it was alive," he said. Nine-month-old Tiffany Sarabia had ridden the wave of mud that swept her from her cot and into the night. Segraves handed the baby to a stranger who rushed her to paramedics and she was loaded into an ambulance. Meanwhile, Tiffany's barely-conscious mother Teresa had been loaded onto the same ambulance. When she awoke, she screamed for her baby before discovering her unharmed in the adjoining stretcher. The mudslide had killed two men and demolished three houses.

FORTEAN TIMES has on file many similar examples of miraculous deliverance. A young woman and her two infant sons were lifted out of their mobile home by a tornado in Virginia in July 1996. They flew 50ft (15m) on a mattress and crashed unscathed into a forest.

IN 1992, a tornado packing winds of up to 206mph (418kph) left a 20-mile (13 km) path of destruction in eastern Mississippi. Three people were killed, 57 injured and more than 200 houses destroyed or damaged. Thomas Moody had given up hope of finding his three-month-old son Tanner after the twister ripped through his mobile home in Meridian. Then he heard whimpering and found the child hanging upside down by his night-shirt 8ft (2.4m) up a pine tree. The little boy suffered a broken rib, bruises and torn tendons. Meanwhile, in nearby Murphy, eight-month-old Telisa Cantrell was also thrown from a mobile home. "She was crying," said Anthony Glass, who found her. "That's the only way I knew where she was. A mattress squashed her against the ceiling. There wasn't a scratch on her."

CURTIS VANCE and his wife lost most of their possessions when a tornado raked the town of Florence, Mississippi, on the night of 21 November 1992. Vance heard the storm coming and went into the bedroom of their mobile home to grab his daughter Selisa, just six days old. "There was a big 'boom' and I was just spinning round," he said. The twister had picked up the mobile home and carried it across the street. The family car was upside down. "I lifted my wife over the pasture fence. We were both looking for the baby," said Vance. He raced down the street to get a torch from a relative, but still the baby was nowhere in sight. The parents were joined by Mrs Vance's aunt, Mary Mayberry, and after 40 minutes of searching, they heard crying. Lightning flashed and Mayberry found baby Selisa in a thicket under a tree. She was unhurt except for two scratches on her face.

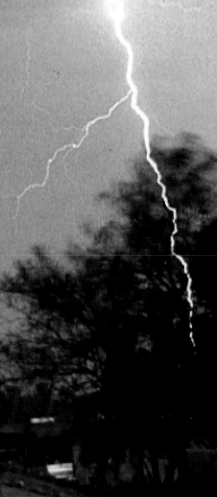

LINES IN THE SAND

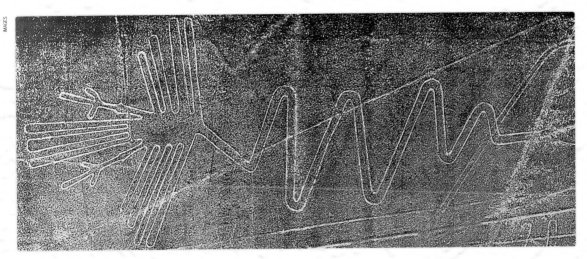

The vast drawings on Peru's famous Nazca plateau have been one of the most enduring of mysteries. Numerous theories have been advanced to explain both their presence and their stunning imagery, but none has found widespread acceptance. One of the more contentious, advanced by Erich von Däniken and others, is that the lines are either "landing strips" for alien spacecraft, or were produced by spaceship exhausts. A further puzzle – one which von Däniken used as evidence for his theories – came in the shape of a number of small, elongated skulls found in burial chambers near the lines. Now, a British team of researchers and academics claims to have come up with a definitive explanation.

The lines were drawn over a 1,000-year period, beginning in the 4th century BC, and show a variety of animals and geometric shapes, some up to 300 feet (98m) high. They were revealed to the modern world in 1926 when pilots first flew over the plain, with further patterns being discovered in the 1950s by German archæologist Maria Reiche, who died earlier this year after a lifetime recording and studying the lines.

The latest five-person team – led by Newcastle University archæologist Dr Tony Spawforth – spent their time studying the lines and various other artefacts associated with the area, examining them for evidence to support each of the various theories they had encountered. Eventually, they came to the conclusion that the lines had originally served as part of a futile attempt to bring rain to the plateau.

Spawforth says that his team were careful not to discount any theory, even von Däniken's, without looking at the evidence. Von Däniken fell early; many of his "landing strips" run up hillsides. Moreover, the straight lines were not peculiar to the plateau, but could be found all over Peru, and appeared to have some ritual significance. Other evidence, such as apparently shamanic paintings on shards of pottery found in and around the plateau, also pointed to a ritual purpose for the lines.

Eventually, Piers Vitebsky, an expert in shamanism and a member of Spawforth's team, was dispatched to show copies of the pictures to a shaman in the Peruvian rainforest. To his surprise, the shaman immediately recognised the animals as shamanic spirit companions; the lines, he explained, were designed to be seen from the sky during shamanic "flight". This still left the question of why they had been executed on such an enormous scale.

A large number of the lines point towards the Andes, which is the area's only source of water. It is estimated that the plain has not seen significant rainfall since the Ice Age. Analysis of mountain ice has shown that the area once experienced a 40-year drought, at roughly the same time that Nazca pottery records a lengthy period of warfare and human sacrifice. Spawforth envisages great lines of shamans, proceeding along the lines while performing rain-bringing rites, "like a vast sacred conga line". The pointed skulls, meanwhile, are most likely down to the South American habit of binding infants' skulls between boards.

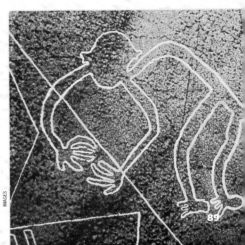

SWAMP GAS

If anyone were to take a survey, there's a fair chance that the first words most people speak after a weird experience are "What the hell was that?" As it happens, there are a lot of people out there who think they know... **JOE McNALLYW** investigates.

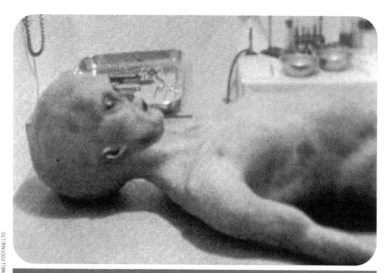

ROSWELL FOOTAGE LTD.

ROSWELL: Did aliens really crash-out in New Mexico or is it just a load of old balloons?

You might expect that the good folk at *Fortean Times* hate it when their favourite UFO or lake monster is explained by some high-and-mighty authority. Not so; in fact these explanations often appear more dubious than the phenomena themselves.

Inevitably, one of the most fertile areas for bizarre explanations has been ufology. Like believers, skeptics tend to exercise their imaginative muscles more often and with more glee than seems entirely healthy. At some time almost anything that takes place in the air has been advanced as an explanation for UFOs. From – inevitably – swamp gas to geese flying in formation, if it's bright and in the air, somebody has used it as a non-paranormal explanation for some sighting or other.

Probably the most controversial series of explanations offered for a supposed UFO event has been the American government's ongoing attempts to put the Roswell "saucer crash" to bed once and for all. Their case hasn't been helped by the fact that they themselves seem unable to settle on a story for what took place.

One of the main planks in the canonical Roswell story is the discovery of debris on remote farmland by rancher William Brazel, generally agreed by researchers to have contained some kind of "tin foil" and pieces of metal or plastic with odd markings on them.

To believers, there are clear signs of alien involvement. To the US military, however, they were for many years "balloon debris" from Project Mogul, a military experiment involving high-altitude balloons. The "mysterious" silver foil, they said, was simply lightweight plastic, while the odd markings were no more than a pattern printed on adhesive tape used to assemble the balloons. This overlooked the fact that no Mogul balloon launches had been pinned down conclusively to the crash date, but hey, you can't have everything.

However, as media interest around Roswell mushroomed in the run-up to 1997's 50th anniversary of the crash, the government felt pressed to proffer yet a further explanation: crash test dummies. Almost entirely contradicting their previous claims, the incident was now said to have been inspired by some sort of retrieval exercise, involving parachuting dummies dropped from aeroplanes. These were the "bodies" witnesses claimed to have seen at the crash site. Oddly, this seemed to convince even fewer people than the Project Mogul story.

Mis-identification of aviation lights and suchlike is probably the most common explanation for sightings given by skeptics and authorities; Allan Hendry's *The UFO Handbook* features a lengthy

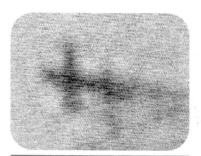

CONGO: Brontosaurus or water boatmen?

section on mis-identifications, and cites dozens of cases where advertising planes and blimps were reported as UFOs.

The description "it looked like the saucers you read about…" is ascribed to "a small National Weather Service balloon"; "[it was] just like the UFO pictures in [the] paper" turned out to be "[a] distant aircraft at sunset"; a UFO which "zigzagged" is "a star seen for forty minutes in one basic position"; and so on. Hendry also identifies a few more unlikely culprits, including floating rafts of spiders' webs catching the sunlight.

One of the most colourful UFO "contactees" is a one-armed Swiss farmer named Billy Meier. For decades Meier has claimed regular contact with space beings from the Pleiades, who meet with him and pass on tit-bits of cosmic wisdom in curiously stilted conversations. One of the more unusual aspects of Meier's contacts is that he has released dozens of astonishingly clear photographs showing enormous saucer-shaped craft manoeuvring in the skies above his farm. American journalist Kal Korff became interested in Meier's case, and began investigating further. Korff is not an out-and-out debunker, but instead holds that some UFO phenomena are real, and works on the principal that this makes it even more important to expose the fakers. After spending some time with Meier and the small, loose band of "followers" who dwell on his farm, Korff came to the conclusion that Meier was a fraud, producing fake photos and phoney insights.

For some time, Meier had been circulating photographs of "Asket", a beautiful young woman in exotic clothes who he claimed was a Pleiadian emissary. Korff spent some years trying to track down the source of this picture, and eventually found it: Dean Martin. The lady identified as "Asket" was a dancer on one of Martin's shows for American television in the 1970s.

Meier proffered his own explanation for this apparent anomaly, showing that it's not just hard-core skeptics who find themselves engaged in astonishing mental gymnastics. The Pleiedians contacted him and set out in great detail exactly how things had come to this sad pass. Firstly, they told Meier that they had warned him about the photo of Asket some years ago, but that he had forgotten about it. They had told him, they went on, that although he had genuinely photographed his Pleiadian friend, he had never received the photo. Instead, as soon as he sent it to be developed, the machinery of the Conspiracy had swung into action. The pictures were intercepted by the Men in Black, a suitable lookalike was discovered – the Dean Martin dancer – and a photograph of her in identical costume and pose was substituted. Meier now realised that he had never had a photograph of "Asket". All this, of course, was simply another attempt to bring Meier into disrepute.

Cryptozoology too seems to have its fair share of strange explanations. There are many people out there willing to accept almost anything apart from the existence of genuine large unknown animals; some have even gone so far as to suggest that the Loch Ness Monster and its kin may be the ghosts of large marine reptiles (which at least disposes of the long-standing niggle over just what it is that the damned things eat).

As with UFOs, there is an awful tendency to debunk at a distance. While criticising a recent Norwegian survey of a supposedly monster-haunted lake, one Oslo Museum zoologist paused to debunk another sighting from the 1880s.

Locals near a lake – which he identifies only as "in Western Norway" – claimed to have seen a large, black, stinking creature, shaped like a snake, break the surface of the lake before disappearing back down to the depths. This, said Torfinn Örmen, "was simply an accumulation of sawdust from the sawmills, mixed with algae from the lake. Methane gas developed in this tangled mass, causing it to float up to the surface. When the ill-smelling gas was released, the 'serpent' sank back down into the water."

THERE IS AN AWFUL TENDENCY TO DEBUNK AT A DISTANCE

SPOT THE DIFFERENCE: Alien babe (top L) or Dean Martin dancing girl (top R, bottom L, R)?

Most alleged lake monster videos which come our way certainly seem to be of waves, but one which came appeared some months ago seemed a little more promising; it showed something large and crocodile-shaped moving very quickly through the water of a reputedly monster-infested Pacific lake. At least one leading cryptozoologist - who shall remain nameless – confided in the authors that it looked to him like nothing so much as a dead crocodile being dragged behind a boat. Similarly, video film which appears to show a brontosaurus-like dinosaur in a lake in the Congo has often been condemned as simply showing two men in a canoe.

Ghosts and the supernatural clearly offer enormous potential both for fraud and for outlandish explanations. One suggestion occasionally floated by skeptics is that a freshly-filled grave will be slightly warmer than the surrounding earth, attracting swarms of midges. These, it is said, might be mistken for a shadowy, ghostly form hovering over the grave.

Mediumship similarly offers a wealth of possibilities. Probably the most famous book attempting to debunk the whole profession is *The Psychic Mafia* by former medium Lamar Keene. Keene – tinged by the near-fanatacism which only seems to afflict the converted – lays bare what he says are the standard tricks used to dupe the elderly, wealthy and gullible into handing over their cash. According to Keene, the entrance hall to any spititualist establishment will be a veritable array of parabolic microphones, designed to catch any useful personal details uttered by the faithful. Worse, Keene says that mediums are more than happy to raid the houses of the recently-deceased in the hope of turning up some

astonishing detail with which to further convince the living – or even cash and valuables.

The ghost hunter Harry Price investigated the medium Helen Duncan (see pp 74-75) and reached some remarkable conclusions. Her spectacular apparitions were not ectoplasm, but wet muslin concealed in a "double stomach", held together with safety pins. Parapsychologist Richard Wiseman regularly stages Victorian-style "séances" in which objects marked with luminous paint fly

WHAT THEY HAD WAS A POP VIDEO BY THE BAND PSYCHIC TV

ALEX HOWE/E. GILFILLAN

around a conveniently darkened room. He achieves these effects through the high-tech medium of a long stick. Some of the most extraordinary revelations have come in the investigation of so-called Satanic Ritual Abuse (SRA). Belief in SRA led to literal witchunts throughout Britain and America in the 1980s; investigators would produce as evidence lurid video recordings, or tales of dark midnight ceremonies where children are sarificed and eaten.

Sadly, the truth was often rather more prosaic. When Channel 4's *Dispatches* programme broadcast a terrifying exposé of a "satanic abuse" cult in England, their evidence initially looked strong. They had what they claimed was

a video of a series of acts of ritual abuse of a particularly vile nature. In fact it was a pop video by the band Psychic TV, introduced by the late underground film-maker Derek Jarman, definitely not involving children at any stage. The programme's chief witness, a woman who claimed that part of the video showed a forced abortion being performed on her, was examined by doctors and found never to have been pregnant.

In the Orkney SRA case, reports of sinister woodland rituals emerged. A figure in black would make children dance around him in a ring as terrifying "occult" music played, and would choose his sacrifices by reaching out with a magical staff. The man in black turned out to be the local vicar; the "satanic" music was from Holst's Planets suite.

Finally, from the opposite extreme, a tale of mind control and worse. The US military is long-rumoured to have carried out experiments in mind-power and time-travel at Montauk. One "exposé" of the project – Commander X's *Incredible Technologies of the New World Order* – reveals just why the project was shut down. Not because it simply didn't work, but because... well, let's let X take over. The project, he says, managed to build a working "Time Tunnel", just like the one in the TV series. "They had a situation where a 'monster from the id' type creature came through and everyone panicked as it ate people and equipment. They had to go back and shut down the unit in Philadelphia in order to shut off the unit in the future so they could stop this creature in 1983..." X's witness also complains that the project's evil bosses would use their time-travel technology to ensure that he returned from his missions just before he left, so that he never stopped work. If the bosses of the world get wind of this, there could be trouble.

1999 ALMANAC

NEVER MISS A STRANGE DAY WITH OUR HANDY GUIDE TO 1999.

JANUARY

1   Circumcisio Domini - Jesus's circumcision.

3   Quadrantid meteors peak.

5   Feast of Simon Stylites, died 459, spent 36 years up a 36 ft pole.

17   St Anthony's day, patron saint of pigs.

21   St Agnes Day, patron saint of sheep.

25   St Paul's Day, today's weather determines the character of the coming year.

FEBRUARY

2   Imbolc, pagan first day of spring. Also Candelmas, watch out, witches about.

3   Feast day of Diana, the huntress.

14   Valentine's Day, traditionally when birds start mating.

MARCH

1   St David's Day, from pagan Dewi, a red sea serpent.

15   Ides of March.

21   Vernal equinox at 01.46am.

24   St Gabriels's Day, brought God's seed to Virgin Mary.

31   Spritualists' Day. 1848, the Fox sisters first heard mysterious knocking sounds in the walls of their home in Hydesville NY.

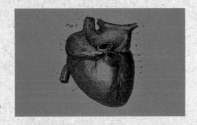

APRIL

1   April Fool's Day.

9   St Casilda's Day, patron saint of dysentry.

16   LSD Day, Albert Hoffman took his bicycle trip, 1943.

19   Aniversaries of the Waco disaster, 1993, and the Oklahoma bombing, 1995.

20   First cuckoo sings today.

22   April Lyrid meteors peak.

23   St George's Day. Was pagan Green Man, spirit of spring.

30   St Sophia's Day. Was spirit of female wisdom, the dove of Aphrodite.

Walpurgisnacht begins at sunset.

MAY

1   Beltane, May Day. Flora and Frey mated in the woods to ensure a fertile spring.

5   May Aquarids peak.

15   St Dymphna's Day, patron saint of the insane.

26   Feast of St Phillip Neri. The pain of his ecstatically swollen heart could be eased only by cooling it on the floor.

JUNE

2   Feast of St Elmo (aka Erasmus). Patron saint of sailors. St Elmo's fire, seen sometimes on the mast of a ship, is a sign of his protection.

13   Feast of St Anthony of Padua, whose corpse exuded the "odour of sanctity", said to work miracles and prevent the body's corruption. Anthony is helpful in finding lost objects.

16   June Lyrid meteors peak.

21   Summer Solstice at 7.49pm.

24   Midsummer Day. Kenneth Arnold saw nine flying crescent-like objects over America's Washington state in 1947.

JULY

7 Consualia, Roman festival for Censos, harvest god. Feast of St Cronaparva, patron saint of dwarves.

9 Feast of St Veronica Giuliani, 17th century visionary and stigmatic.

15 St Swithin's Day. Today's weather determines the temperament of the next 40 years.

22 St Mary of Magdeline's day. Patron saint of prostitutes.

28 July Aquarid meteors peak.

AUGUST

1 Lammas Day, pagan celebration, cutting the first corn.

6 Charles Fort born, 1874.

11 The final total solar eclipse of the millennium, visible form Cornwall, mainland Europe and the Scilly Isles. Could this be the "King of Terror reigning from the skies" prophesied by Nostradamus?

13 Perseid meteors peak.

SEPTEMBER

1 St Fiacre's Day, patron saint of gardeners, also cures piles. Feast of St Giles, patron saint of cripples.

15 Feast Day of St Catherine of Genoa, whose torments included an arm extending five inches.

18 St Joseph of Copertino's Day, the levitating monk.

19 St Janarius' Day. His dried blood still liquifies for an amazed public in Naples Cathedral.

23 Autumn Equinox at 11.31am.

OCTOBER

4 Feast of St Francis of Assisi, spectacular stigmatic.

15 Feast of St Theresa of Avila, ecstatic stigmatic.

16 Feast of St Gerard Majella, who demonstrated bilocation, ESP, healing and prophecy.

21 Orionid meteors peak.

22 The world began today, at 6pm in 4004BC, according to 17th century Bishop James Ussher.

31 Hallowe'en. Once the eve of Samhain, the Grim Reaper. Space and time fracture, allowing contact between the living and the dead.

NOVEMBER

1 All Saints' Day. Originally May 1. Also Samhain, Celtic new year and first day of winter. Fairies and the ghosts of the dead roam the land.

2 All Souls' Day. If dead family members return today, show them some hospitality.

8 Taurid meteors peak.

12 First alleged photo of Nessie taken by Hugh Gray in 1933

17 Leonid meteors peak.

18 Almost 1000 followers of the Reverend Jim Jones killed themselves with a mixture of Kool Aid and cyanide in Guyana, 1978.

22 Feast Day of St Cecilia, patron saint of music.

DECEMBER

6 St Nicholas' Day, the original Santa Claus. Patron saint of pawnbrokers, choirboys, sailors, schoolboys and unmarried maidens

13 St Lucy's Day, protector of the eyes. Hers are often depicted held on a dish.

Gemenid meteors peak.

18 Goth and Saxon period of Yule, known as Yule Girth. Until January 7th.

22 Ursid meteors peak.

Winter Solstice at 7.44am.

25 Christmas Day. According to American prophet Micheal Callagher, the Rapture begins today with the US invasion of Israel.

08/09: Delhi: *South China Morning Post,* 13 Mar 1998. *Brisbane: Courier-Mail (Brisbane),* 2 Feb 1998. Shit hits the fan: *[R],* 10 Mar 1998. Wallaby: *Times,* 19 Feb 1998. Saddam dolls: *D. Telegraph,* 4 Feb 1998. Albin: *[AFP],* 4 Sept. Monk: *[CP],* 10 Sept. Arimanius: *D. Telegraph,* 14 Jun. Buffalo: *[AFP],* 14 Oct. Camera: *Times,* 27 Aug. Loch Ness: *Dundee Courier,* 11 Aug. Trout: *Western Mail,* 24 April 1998. Pastor Stahl: *Wales on Sunday,* 22 Mar 1998. Bees: *D. Telegraph, Guardian,* 16 April 1998. Kakapo: *[R], Times,* 2 April, *D. Telegraph,* 4 April 1998. Crosses: *D. Telegraph,* 12 Aug; *Irish Times,* 13+18 Aug, 8 Sept; *Irish Mirror,* 30 Aug. Elizabeth Decastro: *D. Telegraph,* 3 Jan 1998. HK Statue: *NY Daily News,* 18 Jun. Alien Doctor: *[AFP],* 6 Dec.

10/11: Dr Chen: *Vancouver Sun,* 26 Jun; *Vancouver Province,* 2 July; *Victoria (BC) Times-Colonist,* 7 & 12 July; *South China Morning Post,* 20 July; *D. Telegraph, Independent,* 26 Mar; *Nando Times* 26+31 Mar, 1 April 1998. Moon Sales: *Houston Chronicle,* 27 June. Scorpions *[AP], [R], CNN,* 27 July. Lucia R: *Independent,* 23 Oct. Cotton Buds: *Sunday Telegraph,* 28 Dec. Ross Watt: *Edinburgh Eve News,* 28 Aug. Sherry Moeller: *Hong Kong Standard,* 8 Mar 1998. Man With 3 Tongues: *[R], [AFP],* 8 Mar 1998. Radioactive Woman: *Baltic Times,* 11-17 Dec. Fairies: *Harpers,* Feb 1998.

12: Lourdes Gomez: *[R],* 18 Dec; *D. Mail,* 20 Dec. Chalauy Prathusmasuth: *[R]* 7 Jan 1998. Nuei Thongyai: *S. Mail (Brisbane),* 4 Jan 1998. Ernestine Kieserling: *Guardian,* 3+5 April. Indian Woman: *[AFP],* 22 Oct. Ludwigs: *[AP],* 27 Mar.

13: Tuscany: *D. Telegraph,* 23 Sept; *Times,* 24 Sept. Alan Hinkes: *Independent, Times,* 31 July; *[R],* 5 Aug; *Weekend Telegraph (Australia),* 13 Aug. Pocket Monsters: *Japan Times, Eve. Standard (London),* 17 Dec; *D. Yomiuri,* 18+19+25 Dec; *D. Telegraph,* NY *Times, Guardian, Times, Independent,* 18 Dec; *NY Post,* 18+19 Dec; *NY Daily News,* 18 Dec.

14: See "Dr Chen" references above.

17: Footprints: *Times, Independent, Int. Herald Tribune* 15 Aug; *D. Telegraph,* 16 Aug 1998. Moses: *[AP],* 26 July. Woodhenge: *ITV Teletext, D. Telegraph, Guardian, Times,* 11 Nov.

20: Treacle Mines: *Exeter Express & Echo,* 23 Sept, 2+30 Oct.

24: Al Niño: *Independent,* 3 Mar; *D. Telegraph,* 4 Mar 1998. Kim Lee Chong: *Sun,* 28 Jan 1998. Hitlers: *D. Telegraph,* 17 Feb; *Mirror,* 21 Feb; *Independent,* 5 Mar 1998. Mark Gallagher: *Mirror,* 4 Mar 1998. Prison: *The People,* 21 Sep. Video: *Suffolk Express,* 7 Nov. Detectives: *D. Telegraph,* 11 May 1998. Trees: *Newcastle Journal,* 7 April 1998. Fiats: *Northern Echo,* May. Tug-O-War: *[R], [AP].* 26 Oct.

25: Pigeons: *Express,* 14 May. Daniel Bowden: *USA Today,* 5 June. David Hindmarsh: *[AP],* 11 June. Rosie Lee Hill: *[AP],* 6 Mar. Stephen King II: *Boston Sunday Herald,* 20 April, *Hong Kong Standard,* 27 May. Speed: *[R],* 16 April. Israeli Thief: *Times, Hong Kong Standard,* 8 April. Paco Bocconini: *D. Record,* 21 June. Barry Parks: *Hampshire Chronicle,* 16 May. Sidonia Williams: *NY Daily News,* 8 May.

26/27/28: Hashiem Zayed: *[AP],* 25 July. Tony Wheeler: *[R], D. Telegraph,* 19 Aug. Window Dresser: *D. Mail,* 23 Aug. Vernon Suckerlog: *Scotsman,* 18 July; *D. Star,* 19 July; *Sunday Sport, People,* 20 July. Mark Anthony: *South London Press,* 27 Aug. Rolande Geneve: *Mirror,* 4 July. Otto the Rottweiler: *Guardian,* 11 Dec 1996. Tom Gray: *Mirror,* 8 Aug. Daniel Edwards: *The Citizen (S. Africa),* 1 Sept. Christopher Sean Payne: *Sydney D. Telegraph,* 3 Oct. Anton Crudsch: *People,* 12 Oct. Ouma Hendricks: *[AP],* 29 Dec. Accountant: *[R],* 3 Dec. Choked: *D. Record,* 22 Aug. Marlon Pistol: *People,* 26 Oct. Drowned: *D. Mail,* 22 Oct. Gina Lalapola: *D. Record,* 30 Aug. Elephants: *D. Telegraph,* 7 Nov. Felipe Ortiz: *D. Mail,* 17 Mar. Tamagotchi: *[R],* 8 April 1998. Pilgrims: *[AP],* 9 April 1998. Batshit: *[AFP],* 5 April 1998. Geoff Birch: *Evening Standard,* 15 April 1998.

29: Geronimo: *[R],* 6 Mar, 4 Oct. Chaudhari: *Aberdeen Eve. Express,* 29 July 1996; *Express, D.Mail,* 12 Feb; *D.Mail, Mirror, D.Record,* 12 Feb; *D.Telegraph, Guardian,* 21 April 1998. Geronimo: *[R]* 6 Mar, 4 Oct. Hussein: *[CNN],* 7 Mar, *D.Mail,* 3 April, *[R]* 16 April. Meilleur: *Toronto Globe, Sault Star,* 15 Aug, *North Bay (Ontario) Nugget,* 30 Aug; *D.Telegraph,* 18 April 1998. Mortensen: *Guardian,* 6 Aug; *San Francisco Chronicle,* 17 Aug; *St Louis Post-Dispatch,* 28 April 1998.

34/35: Shot computer: *Guardian,* 14 Aug; *Computer Weekly,* 21 Aug. Liger: *[R],* 25 Sept. My Twinn(tm): *Sunday Mail (Brisbane),* 13 July. Lauretta Adams: *[AP],* 18 Oct. Whistling gunman: *Sunday Mail,* 8 Feb 1998. Bearded lady: *D. Telegraph,* 27 Feb 1998. Georgina Jackson: *NY Post,* 24 July; *Irish Times,* 5 June; *D. Mail,* 16 Aug. Maureen Wilcox: *Focus,* Jan 1998. Self-castration: *Spokane (WA) Spokesman-Review,* 13 Dec; *Wellington (NZ) Evening Post,* 10 May. Michael Zanakis: *D. Telegraph, D. Mail,* 19 Dec. Mike Babone: *NY Post,* 18 Oct. Mormons: *PA,* 10 April 1998. Philip Johnson: *Guardian,* 5 Feb 1998.

36/37: Squirrel: *D. Mail,* 22 Sept. Globster: *Independent, Eastern Daily Press,* 15 Jan 1998. Rattlesnakes: *Seattle Times,* 18 Sept. Sludge Mutant: *Anderson (IN) Herald Bulletin,* 5 Mar. Cats: *St. Petersburg (FL) Times,* 28 Mar; *Edmonton (Alberta) Journal,* 5 Mar; *[AP],* 15 Mar 1998. Chicks: *D. Telegraph,* 2 April 1998. Giant Boa: *[AP],* 10 Aug; *Glasgow Herald,* 12 Aug; *San Francisco Chronicle,* 13 Aug. Ice Worms: *Houston Chronicle,* 1 Aug; *Times,* 4 Aug; *New Scientist,* 9 Aug; *Guardian,* 12 Aug. Albino Penguin: *Guardian,* 12 April.

40: Drunken Monkeys: *South China Morning Post,* 24 Mar 1998. Monkey Jail: *D Telegraph,* 19 Aug. Macaques: *[AFP],* 28 Jan; *Victoria (BC) Times-Colonist,* 1 Feb 1998. Gorillas: *[AFP],* 23 Oct. Monkey Madness: *[AP],* 18 Mar 1998. Monkey Business: *[AP],* 14 Oct.

41: Scotty: *D. Telegraph,* 30 Dec; *Western Morning News, Western Daily Press,* 31 Dec. Baby: *D. Record, D. Mirror,* 25 Nov 96. Argo: *Verdens Gang (Oslo),* 16 Mar; *Saginaw News (MI),* 17 Mar 95. Roc: *[AP],* 27 June 96. Donna: *Expressen (Sweden),* 11 Jan 1998.

42/43: Doggy Style: *D. Mail,* 7. Nov. Lobsters: *[R],* 14 Nov; *D. Mail,* 15 Nov; *NY Times,* 16 Nov; *Doncaster Star,* 18 Dec; *Independent, Guardian, D. Mail,* 9 Dec. Black Leopard: *D. Mail,* 28 July. Gwan: *Guardian, Times, D. Mail,* 12 Nov. Frogs: *[R],* 17 Nov; *Minneapolis (MN) Star-Tribune,* 21 Nov; *Irish Times,* 15 Jan 1998. Pig: *[AP], Middlesbrough Eve. Gazette,* 14 April 1998; *Santa Barbara (CA) News-Press,* 17 April 1998.

44: Elk: *Sydvenska Dagbladet, Expressen,* 14 Nov. Elephants: *[R],* 29 Dec. Rats: *London Eve. Standard,* 1 Feb 93; *D Telegraph,* 24 Dec. Drunken Rats: *New Scientist,* 7 Jan, 13 May 95. Wax Wings: *[AP],* 8 Nov,. Crows: *Guardian,* 5 July 94.

45: See "Globster", above.

46/47: [All except where stated] WMN = *Western Morning News;* WDP = *Western Daily Press* BUCKS: *Milton Keynes Citizen,* 27 Feb, 14 Aug, 6 Nov, 23 Dec; *Milton Keynes Herald,* 28 Mar, 12 Dec; *Milton Keynes S. Citizen,* 24 Aug, 14 Dec; CORNWALL: *Plymouth Eve. Herald,* 18 Jan, 28+29 Nov, 3+8 Dec; *WMN,* 21 Jan, 15 May, 30 Aug, 18+21+22 Oct, 5+8+10+14+15+17+18+28 +29 Nov, 2+6+12+27+30 Dec; *Cornish Guardian,* 23 Jan, 22 May, 23 Oct, 6+13+20+27 Nov, 4+11 Dec; *West Briton,* 1+22 May, 23 Oct; *Cornishman,* 22+29 May, Nov, 4 Dec; *D.Telegraph,* 18 Oct; *Bristol Eve. Post,* 18 Oct; *Wolverhampton. Express & Star,* 18 Oct; *Local Govt. Chronicle,* 24 Oct; *S. Times,* 16 Nov; *S. Express,* 16 Nov; *Independent,* 17 Nov; *WDP,* 17 Nov; *Express, D.Mail, Exeter Express & Echo,* 28 Nov; *Mirror,* 23 Dec. CAMBS: *Cambs Eve. News,* 22 Feb, late Oct; *Weekend Telegraph,* 8 Mar. DERBYS: *DerbyEve. Telegraph,* 22 Mar; *Peak Advertiser,* 30 June; *Burton Mail,* 22 Oct, 22 Dec. DEVON: *Kennet Star,* 23 Jan; *WMN,* 2 April, 12 Nov, 4 Dec; *North Devon Journal,* 10 April, 20 Nov; *Express & Echo,* 11+20+29 Nov; *D.Telegraph, Times,* 18 Nov; *North Devon Gazette,* 20 Nov. DORSET: *Dorset Eve. Echo,* 10 May, 5 June. ESSEX: *Epping & Ongar Gazette,* 13 Mar; *Southend Eve. Echo,* 13 May, 14 Aug, 3 Nov; *Braintree Chronicle,* 30 May; *News of the World,* 1 June; *Chelmsford Yellow Advertiser,* 6 June, 11 July; *Thurrock Gazette,* 6+13+27 June; *D.Mail,* 18 June; *East Anglian Daily Times,* 22 Oct; GLOS: *WDP,* 10 Jan; *Citizen (Gloucester),* 29+30

Jan, 18+20 Aug. HANTS: *News (Portsmouth),* 17 Mar, 10 April; *Southampton Daily Echo,* 17 Mar 2+8+20 Oct; *New Forest Post,* 20 Mar, 31 July; *Haslemere Herald,* 20 June; *Lymington Times,* 22 Nov. HEREFORD & WORCS: *Hereford Times,* 9 Jan; *WDP,* 14 Feb; *Shropshire Star,* 11 April. HERTS: *Barnet & Whatstone Press,* 20 Aug. KENT: *Kent Today,* 16 Jan, 4 Feb, 5 Mar, 25+27+28 Nov, 8 Dec; *Kentish Gazette,* 16 May. LANCS: *Southport Visiter [sic],* 24 Jan; *Formby Times,* 30 Jan; *Formby Champion,* 2 April; *Bury Times,* 5 April. LEICS: *Times,* 8 Aug; personal communication. LINCS: *Lincs Echo,* 18+23 April. GREATER MANCHES-TER: *Stockport Times,* 10 July; *Manchester Metro News,* 11 July. *Eastern Daily Press,* 22 Feb, 26 Mar, 6 May, 5+24 June, 4+7+8+24 July, 4+30+31 Oct, 21 *Eastern Eve. News,* 24 Feb, 26 Mar, 26+28 April, 5 June, 3+7+8+18+23+26 July, 6+14+21+23+25 Aug, 2 Sept; *Wymondham & Attleborough Mercury,* 10 Oct; *Times,* 1 Dec; *Independent,* 3 Dec. NORTHANTS: *Kettering Eve. Telegraph,* 4 Jan, 28 Mar, 15 April, 5 May, 7+11+23 June, 7 July, 27+29 Oct, 20+21 Nov; *Corby Eve. Telegraph,* 9 April, *Northampton Chronicle & Echo,* 28 Oct, 4 Nov. NORTHUMBER-LAND: *Northumberland Gazette,* 31 Oct. OXON: *Kent Today,* 25 Mar; *Oxford Mail,* 2 Aug, 16 Nov. RUTLAND: *Leicester Mercury,* 10+14 Mar, 21 May. SALOP: *Shropshire Star,* 21 Feb, 14 April, 19 Sept; *Bridgnorth Journal,* 21 Feb, 19 Dec; *Shropshire Journal,* 11 April; *Shropshire Chronicle,* 2 Oct; *Wolv. Express & Star,* 29 Nov. SOMERSET: *D.Telegraph,* 19 Jan; *WDP,* 19 July; *Bristol Eve. Post,* 25 Aug. STAFFS: *Wolv. Express & Star,* 26+27 Aug. SUFFOLK: *Eve. Star (Ipswich),* 23 Jan; *Eastern Daily Press,* 25 April. SURREY: *Haslemere Herald,* 13+26+27 June, 4+18+31 July; *County Border Times & Mail,* 17 June; *Walton & Weybridge Informer,* 22 Aug; *Surrey Advertiser,* 29 Aug. SUS-SEX: *Brighton Eve. Argus,* 27 Mar, 14 June, 15 July; *D.Mail, Express,* 10 April; *Midhurst & Petworth Observer,* 19 June, 11 Sept; *Hastings Observer,* 18+25 July; *Littlehampton Gazette,* 15 Aug; *West Sussex County Press,* 17 Oct; *Sussex Express,* 31 Oct, 7+28 Nov. WEST MIDLANDS: *Wolv. Express & Star,* 25 Nov; *Stourbridge Chronicle,* 28 Nov. WILTS: *Swindon Eve. Advertiser,* 16 Jan; *Gazette & Herald (Marlborough),* 23 Jan. WORCS: *Wolv. Express & Star,* 16 Sept; *Worcester Eve. News,* 13 Oct. YORKS: *Dewsbury Reporter,* 10+17+31 Jan; Hull Daily Mail, 4 Feb; *Scarborough Eve. News,* 10+22 Feb; *Northern Echo,* 11 Feb; *D.Telegraph, Times,* 12 Feb; *Sheffield Star,* 24 May, 16 Aug; *Barnsley Independent,* 9 July. IRELAND: *News Letter (Belfast),* 23 Jan; *Irish Times,* 28 April; *Belfast Telegraph,* 16 Aug. SCOTLAND: *Scotland on Sunday,* 12 Jan; *Edin. Eve. News,* 16 Jan, 7+11 Mar, 7 April, 2+21+22 May, 9+23 July, 26 Sept; *Dundee Courier & Advertiser,* 17 Jan, 26 Sept, 27 Oct, 17+19 Nov, 19 Dec; *Glasgow Herald,* 21 Jan, 16 Nov; *Sun,* 8 Mar, 24 Sept; *Aberdeen Eve. Express,* 24+31 Mar, 120 April, 10+17 June, 17 Oct; *S. Mail,* 25 May, 1+15 June; *Carlisle Eve. News*

& Star, 17 July; *Falkirk Herald,* 24 July; *Border Telegraph,* 5 Aug, 14 Oct; *D.Record,* 3 Oct; *Mearns Leader (Kincardineshire),* 24+31 Oct; *Scotsman,* 17 Nov; *Fife Free Press,* 21 Nov; *Dundee Eve. Telegraph,* 10 Dec. WALES: *D.Post,* 6 Jan, 13 Feb, 20 May; *D.Mail,* 14 Jan; *Brecon & Radnor Express,* 22+30 Jan; *Western Mail,* 12 Feb, 29 Mar, 5 April, 3 May, 11 Dec; *Wolv. Express & Star,* 13 Feb; *Mirror,* 14 Feb; *Guardian, Times,* 4 April; *Independent,* 5 April; *Observer,* 6 April; *Heart of Wales Chronicle,* 7 April; *Wales on Sunday,* 15 April, 8 June; *News of the World,* 31 Aug; *S. Mirror,* 31 Aug; *Liverpool Daily Post,* 18 Nov.

48/49: Tortoise: *Times, D. Telegraph, Express,* 18 Aug. Armadillos: *Times,* 15 Sept. Frog: *Victoria (BC) Times-Colonist,* 13 Sept. Falcon: *London Evening Standard,* 23 July. Tamagotchi: *[AP],* 25 Nov. Duck: *[AFP],* 22 Nov. Roaches: *North Bay (Ontario) Nugget,* 20 Dec. Parakeet: *Wolverhampton Express & Star,* 25 Feb; *Trowbridge (Wilts) Star,* 5 Mar 1998.

50/51: Cricket: *S. Telegraph,* 6 July. Lille: *Guardian,* 17 Sept. Library: *Times,* 17 Sept. Juan Villasante: *[All 1998] Irish Times, Guardian,* 7 Feb; *S. Times,* 15 Feb; *Independent,* 27 Feb. Mermaid: *[All 1998] D. Telegraph,* 7+8+10 Jan, 5+6 Feb; *[AP],* 8 Jan, 5 Feb; *[R],* 9 Jan; *Guardian,* 10 Jan. "Spies": *Guardian,* 16 Oct. Suzanna Borg: *D. Mail,* 4 April 1998. Iolantha Bauer: *D. Telegraph,* 18 April 1998.

52/53: "Hot pants": *D. Telegraph,* 14 Aug; *D. Mail, Halifax Eve. Courier,* 15 Aug. Voodoo: *CNN,* 11 Sept. Elvis: *[AP, R], Scotsman,* 12 Aug. Bells: *Sydsvenskan,* 4 Oct. Vampire Mummies: *Jakarta Post,* 23 Sept. Gemma Harris: *Southend Eve. Echo,* 8 July. Fr Critch: *Victoria (BC) Times-Colonist,* 13 April 1998. Fires: unknown, via Scott Corrales. Witches: *[AP],* 5 Jan 1998. PC Janaway: *Times, Mirror,* 13 April.

56/57: Daniel Geraghty: *Sheffield Star,* 25 Oct, 10 Nov; *D. Mail, Yorkshire Post,* 12 Nov. Ghost Tax: *D. Telegraph,* 27 Aug. St Mark's Ghost: *Church Times,* 5 Dec. Peterhouse: *D. Telegraph, D. Mail, Wolverhampton Express & Star,* 19 Dec; *Independent,* 20 Dec; *Times Higher Education Supplement,* 19 Dec, 2 Jan 1998. Lady Lovibund: *[All 1998] S. Telegraph,* 1 Feb; *Thanet Times,* 10 Feb; *D. Mail, Kent Messenger, Isle of Thanet Gazette,* 13 Feb; *Guardian, Express,* 14 Feb. Thanks to Tom Perrott of the Ghost Society.

61: Grab: *[All 1998] Independent,* 22 Feb; *BBC News website,* 24 Feb; *[AP],* 1 Mar. Audrey Santo: *S. Express,* 16 Nov. Danielle O'Connor: *S. People,* 22 June.

69: St Joseph: *Austin American-Statesman,* 22 June; *Int. Herald Tribune,* 25 Aug. Nun: *[AP]* 24 April 1994. Eclipse: *[R],* 18 Sept. Virgin: *Middle East Times,* 5+18 Sept; *[AP]* 14 Sept.

74/75: Helen Duncan: *Psychic News,* 1 Oct;

Portsmouth News, 2 Oct; *S. Telegraph,* 5 Oct. African Witchcraft: *Times of Zambia,* 3+4 April 1998. Zombies: *The West Australian,* 8 Oct.

76/77: Iranian stories: *Hamshahri and Gomhori (Iran),* April. Cremation: *Hong Kong Standard,* 11 Dec. Lost tribe: *Toronto Globe & Mail,* 31 Jan 1998. Kalyani Thapa: *The Rising Nepal,* 30 Dec, 12 Jan 1998; *Spotlight,* 9 Jan 1998; *Kathmandu Post,* 12 Jan 1998. Crucifixion: *Independent, Newcastle Journal,* 9 April 1998; *[AP]* 10 April 1998. Shrieking woman: *Times,* 15 Oct. Korea: *[AP],* 29 Sept. Taliban: *D. Telegraph, Times,* 7 Oct.

78/79: Cataract River: *New Scientist,* 16 Aug. Seaweed: *Guardian,* 18 Aug. Jelly: *Hungarian Public Radio,* 20 Jun; *Scotland on Sunday,* 27 July. Puffball: *Middlesbrough Eve. Gazette,* 1 Aug; *Yorkshire Post, D. Mail,* 20 Sept. Clouds: *D. Telegraph,* 23 Sept. Meteorite: *D. Mail,* 17 Dec. Ice storm: no reference. P. piscicidia: *University of Charleston Aquatic Botany Lab website,* no date. Stumps: *S. Mail (Brisbane),* 15 Mar 1998. Lightning: *Times,* 17 April 1998.

84/85: Skywriting: *Guardian,* July 1998. David Lee: *D. Mail, Express,* 4 May 1998. Leonids: *The Record (Hackensack, NJ),* 18 Nov; *NY Daily News,* 18+21 Nov. Kostroma: *Vancouver Sun,* 7 June. Chicago: *UPI, UFO UpDates* 3 Dec. Greenland: *Independent,* 16+17 Dec; *Times, D. Mail, Sun,* 17 Dec; *Seattle Times,* 22 Dec. Sydney: *D. Telegraph (Sydney),* 8 Dec.

88: [All 1998 except where stated] *San Francisco Examiner,* 23 Feb; *Orlando Sentinel,* 24 Feb; *NY Post, D. Telegraph,* 25 Feb; *Times-Picayune (New Orleans),* 12 Mar 1992; *[AP, R],* 25 Nov 1992; *S. Mail,* 4 Aug 1996; *Orange County Register (Santa Ana, CA),* 25 Feb.

89: Australian outback figure: *Guardian,* July 1998; Nazca: S. *Times,* 17 Aug.

All references are for 1997, excepet where stated.

WEIRDNESS THE WHOLE YEAR ROUND

FOR A MONTHLY FIX OF WEIRDNESS PICK UP FORTEAN TIMES AT ALL GOOD NEWSAGENTS

SUBSCRIPTION & AVAILABILITY INFORMATION: 01454 620070

TO CONTACT THE FORTEAN TIMES TEAM, WRITE TO FORTEAN TIMES, BOX 2409, LONDON NW5 4NP